The Ultimate Book of
Power Kiting and
Kiteboarding

Acknowledgments
Navigator Guides would like to thank all those at
Flexifoil International for the enormous contribution
they have made to the publishing of this book, but
a special mention to Jeremy Pilkington for the intro-
duction to Jeremy Boyce, an inspired choice of
writer, Jane Rankin for all her help and to Andrew
Jones and Mike Shaw for their technical advice and
input. Likewise, Paul Thody from Air Born Kites,
Matt Taggart from Ozone Kites and J from ATB
Mag. for special technical advice.
Special thanks for use of photography go to Wipika,
Naish (Courtesy of Naish International. © 2004
Stephen Whitsell), Ozone, Gaastra (S. Whitesell
and M. Ribkoff), Dan Eaton and Dave Stratton at
Powerkiteshop.com, Cabrinha Kitesurfing,
Slingshot (John Bilderbeck and Dan Gavere), Libre,
Peter Lynn, Ballistic, New Tech, Bob Childs and
Takoon.

Design: Smith, Cowan and Wilkinson
Illustrations: Liz Johnson
Contributors: Andrew Jones and Mike Shaw
Photographers: Alan Pritchard, Andrew Jones, Carol
Kohen, Christian Black, Dan Eaton, Jono Knight,
John Carter, Ray Merry, Ronny Kiaulehn and Jane
Rankin
Proofreading: Susannah Wight
Colour reproduction: PDQ Digital Media Solutions Ltd
Printed and bound in China

THE ULTIMATE BOOK OF
POWER
KITING
and
Kiteboarding

JEREMY BOYCE

THE LYONS PRESS
Guilford, Connecticut
An imprint of The Globe Pequot Press

Contents

History

It's been nearly 30 years since the development of the first steerable or stunt kites, and over 15 years since the appearance of the first commercially available kite buggy. This heralded the kite traction revolution that has brought power kiting to where it is today, standing on the verge of a breakthrough into the big time, courtesy of the now massively popular buggying and kiteboarding. Like many such sports and leisure pursuits, one company and its innovative product kicked the whole power kite thing off.

The first modern power kite, the Flexifoil Stacker, was conceived, designed, and built in Britain almost 30 years ago by two highly motivated people working from home, a true garden-shed beginning to what has now become a worldwide brand and indeed industry. In many ways the most surprising thing is that it's taken so long for their outstanding invention to grab the popularity it has, triggering so many spin-off activities (from simply flying the kites) along the way.

As with any famous invention it's arguable that someone else would have thought of it if Flexifoil hadn't but, the point is, they did. And it's certainly true that there are now dozens of designers and manufacturers of highly competitive traction kites fueling a rapidly growing industry, such is the current worldwide interest in kite-powered possibilities. You could say that Flexifoil has made possible the whole traction scene as we know it today.

How It All Began

To get the full picture you have to make your way back through the mists of time to the mid-1970s, back to a time when there were no stunt kites of any description to be bought. Then, madcap British inventor Peter Powell came up with his eponymous diamond-shaped, long-tailed stunter – a kite form much imitated since by manufacturers all over the world and popularized in America particularly by Trlby and Ace Kites.

Around the same time, also in Britain, two design students – Andrew Jones and Ray Merry – were experimenting with a series of large-format wind sculptures. They had built a series of sky tubes of increasingly scary dimensions (although they lacked a serious lifting device for them, resorting to long poles and buildings to get them off the ground) before embarking on their ultimate project, an inflatable air-foil wing sculpture that could be tethered as a piece of temporary, movable, public art. Anticipating the computer age, they even mocked up photographs of the Grand Canyon, with their creation superimposed, showing clearly, even at this early stage, the instantly recognizable profile of the Flexifoil power kite wing. Although they

▶ *The originators Ray Merry and Andrew Jones*

started experimenting with wind devices as early as 1972, it wasn't until the late 1970s, after a lengthy series of wind-tunnel tests, that the first Flexifoils appeared, made from polythene with an externally fitted cane leading edge rod, but in essence the same kite that is still manufactured today as the top selling Stacker 6.

What Next?

The kites were an instant success, in the limited terms of reference the kite industry offered at that time. Nevertheless, the concept of using kites for traction began to export itself around the world, establishing links with other windpower freaks around the globe. Among these was New Zealander Peter Lynn. Where Jones and Merry had toyed with the idea of some kind of cart and even boat towed by kites, Lynn advanced the concept several strides when in the mid-1980s he began appearing at kite festivals on a custom designed and built steel-framed kite buggy. His three-wheel design (two rear wheels and a single front steering wheel operated by the feet, leaving hands free to control the kite) established a model that has not been challenged since. A 2004 style kite buggy retains that essential format even if the

details and fittings have evolved somewhat, as you would expect.

At first, control wasn't what it could be and Lynn was notorious for scything through entire kite festivals, taking out kites as he went and leaving a trail of furious kite fliers in his wake. Be that as it may, kite buggying was born and taken up with enthusiasm in many countries. Lynn produced a range of power kites of his own, the Peel series, then designed a production buggy for Flexifoil. All very friendly, even in business. In the mid-1980s Ray Merry left Europe for

▲ *Sky tubes: Early experiments*

water ski, combined with a huge half-moon, rigid-framed, two-lined steerable kite flown from a control bar fitted with motorized line winders, was eerily close to the arched kite shape and (twin-tip) board that have become such big business today. The fact that he'd already perfected his water starts and getting upwind in time to be demoing his rig in 1992–93, five full years before the sport even began to happen, shows how ahead of his time Roeseler was.

Second came the development of new control systems for kites, which made buggying a far more viable possibility and later opened the door to numerous other kite-powered activities, enabling them to flourish to a much greater degree than previously. The four-line control concept was devised at the end of the 1980s by Revolution Enterprises, a San Diego-based company run by the enigmatic Hadziki family, also specializing in the manufacture of high-quality carbon fiber rods for golf clubs, arrow shafts and, yes, kites. Their "Revolution" four-line framed kite and "total control" slogan made their impact on power kite design when first Robert Graham's Quadrifoil company, then Ray Merry's new venture, Cobra Kites, released their Quadrifoil and Skytiger kites, respectively – power kites that used Revolution's four-line total control idea.

America to set up Cobra Kites, a design and manufacture company in its own right but also providing a distribution for Flexifoil kites in America. As the gospel spread, power kiting was slowly growing in popularity but lacked that something that would give it a quantum leap in terms of mass appeal. That process started at the beginning of the 1990s, when two significant steps forward were made in America that would "revolutionize" the power kite world.

It's hard to say which ultimately made the more significant contribution.

The first advance showed a remarkable pioneering spirit and awareness of a possible commercial application that took another decade to come to fruition. The man who first took kites onto the water in a meaningful, not to mention successful, way was in the process of developing the equipment to do so. Cory Roeseler saw the possibility and developed a rig, the Kiteski, that was an early forerunner of what we recognize today as kiteboarding. His single

9

The realization of Lynn-inspired production buggies and the advent of four-line power kites provided the platform for the spectacular growth the industry has seen over the most recent decade. From the beaches where the buggies prospered it seemed a natural next step to take kites onto the water, but Roeseler's rig, interesting though it was, clearly wasn't practical or commercially viable enough. While all this was going on, over in France a pair of sailor–designer–adventurers, the Legaignoux brothers, had been working since the early 1980s on a concept of their own – half-kite, half-sail but, importantly, water re-launchable. They'd intended it to be compatible with a board for surfing but had never refined a working system. The closest they had come was an inflatable canoe to which the kite was anchored in order to drag it over the water. A third Frenchman joined the attack, Manu Bertin, a former world-record holder at speed windsurf and hugely experienced waterman. His determination to succeed at surfing with a kite, the Legaignoux's Wipika kite, was largely responsible for kiteboarding starting when it did. And when Bertin took his rig to Maui, the very epicentre for everything that surfs or boards in the world, for sure the cat was out of the bag. When opinion-forming movers and shakers such as windsurf legends Robby Naish and Pete Cabrinha jumped on board, quickly releasing their own ranges of boards and Wipika-inspired water re-launchable kites, it was clear that power kiting had taken on an altogether new dimension, one that was to move it relatively quickly up into the big league of extreme sports, a destination which, for a long time, it looked as though it might never reach.

Future Perfect

The power kite market in 2004 is a massive free-for-all. Not only have kites gone onto the water, they're increasingly pressed into service on snowboards, snow skis, ice kites, mountain boards, roller blades – basically, anything you can do that moves, someone's going to try it faster, harder and up in the air on the end of a power kite, if they haven't already.

With all those specialisms have come ever more numerous manufacturers, keen for a piece of the action and a slice of the growing market that exists for power kiting in all its weird and wonderful forms. With them, technological input has come from other areas such as sailmaking, windsurfing and paragliding. Competitiveness in the business has driven the rapid development of better and safer equipment, making the sport accessible in a way that it had always dreamed of being. From two blokes in a garden shed in Cambridgeshire to a worldwide industry with dozens of manufacturers, thousands of players, and millions of happy customers.

Interestingly many of those early pioneers are still there, heavily involved in the new aspects of kite power. Jones is still in position at Flexifoil and has seen the company become the single biggest pure power kite manufacturer in the world. Lynn is still going strong down under; Merry's Cobra Kites is alive and kicking in America; Quadrifoil now operates from Switzerland; and the Legaignoux brothers with their Takoon company are in France. Roeseler, too, is still active in the scene, a pro-kiteboard rider and equipment developer for the American sail-making Gaastra company. The power kite scene has moved a long way and swept a lot of people along with it. None of them knew where they were going when they started this thing and there's no telling where it'll go next. As power kite pioneer and Flexifoil co-designer Andrew Jones himself says: "Its just great to use the wind to go somewhere".

In every sense!

"I've jumped out of planes and everything, but for me the buzz you can get from power kites stands on its own – something you have to have a lot of respect for but with big rewards for sure. "

JASON FURNESS Flexifoil-sponsored kiteboarder and demonstrator, ex World Champion kite buggyer, traction junkie

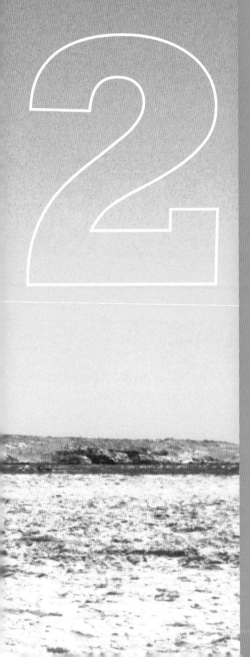

2 Basics

There almost couldn't be anything more simple than flying a two- or four-line stunt or power kite. Think bike riding without the complication of pedaling to keep moving. To control the kite (bike) you move the handles of the control bar push-me-pull-you-style: pull right to turn right, pull left to turn left, hands parallel to go straight. All good kites (sometimes also referred to as wings) come with instructions, but there are all kinds of dos and don'ts that you pick up with experience. They help build your understanding of how the wind and the kites work together to deliver the result you're looking for – endless hours of fun and amusement. It may be simply for pleasure or it might all come together one day to save your own or someone else's life. No amount of instruction books and videos can make you into the perfect pilot because, ultimately, there's no substitute for getting out there and flying.

Once you get a two-line power kite flying you can completely control it and maneuver it exactly where you want it to go. The kite will want to move forwards almost all the time and it's up to your piloting skill both to keep it moving around without crashing into the ground or into any other kites, and to make sure that the flying lines never get so twisted by repeated turns in one direction that you lose all response from the kite. It might sound complicated but it actually requires less mental and physical agility than many everyday activities such as using a cell phone, driving a car, or, as most people seem to prefer, doing both at the same time (this of course is strictly illegal and not recommended).

"People think kites are for kids and wimps 'til they have their first go on a 'serious' power kite and have been dragged all over the beach by it, then you can see them thinking 'Jeez, this thing pulls like a train'. One bite is usually enough to get them running back for more. Power kiting's like that, once you're hooked you can never get enough!"

PETER LYNN power kite and kite buggy pioneer designer

It doesn't stop there as there is also a whole generation of maneuverable traction kites with not just two but four control lines; these are even more sophisticated technically, more controllable. In the right circumstances they can be maneuvered even more precisely to deliver ever-more consistent power and efficiency, and yes, even program your video recorder for you. They have helped take power kiting to where it is today, a sport with many layers of sophistication and enjoyment and general ease of use that explains much of the enormous present day popularity for power and traction kiting as an extreme sport and leisure pursuit. In short, a sport on the verge of greatness.

What Is Power Kiting All About? What's The Crack?

Clearly we would in no way condone anyone flying out of control or attempting any serious traction action before they're properly ready and, even then, under close supervision. Nevertheless, the short answer to the question "what is power

◀ Simple kite maintenance
▶ Flexifoil Super 10

kiting all about?" is, the flying of large single or stacked (several kites linked together) maneuverable kites in such a way as to achieve traction – generally be dragged around, and often above, your chosen flying site by whatever means possible. This can include skidding or skudding (being dragged along on your feet or back), jumping or "getting airs," body surfing, buggying or karting, land-boarding, kiteskating, boating, water skiing, skiing, snowboarding and power kiting's market leader, kiteboarding or kite surfing.

The longer, and somewhat more considered, version of this is that power kiting is all about learning how to use the elements (in this instance the wind and your physical location), in a safe and controlled manner so as to deliver maximum enjoyment with minimum risk. Power kiting qualifies to be listed as an extreme sport – extreme injuries, even death, can occur (and indeed have occurred) if you don't respect and pay proper attention to what you are doing. That starts with looking after yourself and your equipment, and taking note of the weather conditions when you are power kiting. You must be certain that you know what you're doing and that you understand your own limits and those of your equipment. Whatever level

you're doing this at, either for pure recreational pleasure now and then or because you want to be a star rider on the kiteboarding pro tours, you must understand properly how your kite works before you start taking risks. Of course it's accepted that the attraction of extreme sports is the risk and consequent adrenaline rush that comes with it. The trick is whether you succeed in making the risk or not rather than whether you end up in hospital or not.

Successful power kiting involves working out where your limits are and pushing them gradually further and further until you reach your desired level of skill and buzz, which, for many, is what it's all

▲ High-speed buggy wipeout

about. Like a lot of power kiters, you may find that once hooked you can never get enough, always looking for more power and more danger (going faster, jumping higher, and so on). That buzz comes at a price, one you should start paying straightaway by reading the following safety advice rather than paying later in the hospital or, worse still, facing a costly damages lawsuit.

Safety

Walk, Don't Run.
It's vitally important so it's worth repeating until it becomes a mantra: "Safety is the responsibility of the flyer! Safety is the responsibility of the flyer!...".

Just like most other extreme sports, especially if you're going to be taking it up in the air or on water or the sea, you need to totally familiarize yourself with your equipment at the outset. Learn how to control a kite or wing of manageable size properly before you start risking life and limb on any of the large number of serious traction and sport wings on the market today. Once you've learned the basics you'll be ready to get going with some of the big, adrenaline-inducing kites, which serious power kiting is all about. All the same, be ready to be shocked and surprised by just how much "grunt" these wings can generate, and never underestimate what can happen when you start playing around with the elements, such as wind or water. What you take the time to learn today might well save a life tomorrow – your own or that of a colleague.

It's worth remembering that a kite is a sail, just like on a boat, and that the bigger the kite the greater the power it can generate. The risk of personal injury is ever present and, as an opening piece of advice, let's say that if you are one of those people who falls hard and breaks easily then maybe power kiting isn't for you. If, on the other hand, you know how to fall without hurting yourself, and you bounce rather than break, then read on. You will need a reasonable level of fitness if you want to come to grips with the big power generators. If you don't already have good fitness you will need to build it up by flying smaller kites to begin with before moving onwards and upwards, literally and metaphorically. It is easy to tear muscles and tendons, and these injuries take time to mend and will keep you off the flying field for lengthy periods. Broken wrists, ankles and collar bones can too easily result from heavy landings on hard surfaces. In any event, after your first couple of sessions you will find that power kiting works on different muscles and in

◀ The 'Bullet' a quad line power kite

a different way from what you are used to. Expect to feel some aches and pains in unusual places as your body adjusts.

Safety Aids

With the speed of technical innovation there has been in power kiting recently, there are now lots of pieces of equipment and safety aids available to the modern power kiter, in many cases tagged onto the kites (this is especially so in kiteboarding). Harnesses are common in kiteboarding and buggying – without them you couldn't cope with the huge pull of the kites for any length of time. Never, however, under any circumstances, permanently attach yourself to the kite(s). No matter how good and experienced a kite flier you are, the unexpected can always happen and you may need to separate yourself from the kite quickly. Quick releases, de-power systems, flotation jackets, crash helmets, knee and elbow pads, goggles, and so on, are all part of the power kiter's essential equipment nowadays. But never forget that the first level of safety is the flier him or herself. Honesty and awareness about your own skill level and experience, and

understanding your equipment and the conditions on the day, can all save you an immense amount of trouble or injury.

Whatever equipment you've got, you'll need to check it over frequently for wear and tear. Equipment failure at an inopportune moment, especially out on the water or up in the air, could have serious consequences. Take or send equipment back to your dealer or the manufacturer if it is faulty. Many kites and other pieces of equipment are guaranteed against faulty manufacture or unexplained failure. That's not an invitation to trash your kite to bits and expect it to be repaired or replaced free of charge. There are clauses about normal wear and tear in all guarantees and retailers and manufacturers are eagle-eyed. They can spot mistreatment a mile off. Look after your equipment and it will look after you. Carry out repairs without delay. In any event, money spent on a repair could be a life saver and there's no price on that.

Be Aware Of Other People

Safety is more than just a personal issue. A little carelessness or overenthusiasm can mean crashing your kite into or onto spectators and passers-by. While many power kites are, in principle, soft (with no rigid frame parts), they can, as we have said, generate enormous power and cause serious injury. But it's not just the kite itself that can be dangerous. Between you and the kite can be anything up to 45 meters (150 feet) of flying lines, which will be moving through the air under extreme tension. The flying lines are thin, made from high-quality, light-weight materials to reduce drag and make the kites more efficient. This is a potentially fatal combination as, when flying a reasonable-sized power kite, the effect of the pull and tension gives the lines a cutting capability similar to cheese wire. There are countless stories of careless power kiters losing fingertips or severing ears with their flying lines. Always disable your kite and flying lines on the ground when you are not using them.

It is your responsibility as the flyer to make sure you have adequate space for what you are doing. You must allow a clear space downwind of where you're standing at least twice the length of your flying lines to allow for being pulled forward, specially during the launch phase, and a similar amount of space to each side. If people come too close or stand under the kite(s) while you're flying, you must fly your kite

▶ *Control bar and harness, the safe way to handle big power*

to a safe place (at the zenith above your head) and either ask them to move or move yourself until it's safe to fly again. You might want to think about some kind of public indemnity or liability insurance. Many clubs and associations offer this as part of their membership and we recommend that you take out appropriate coverage.

There are some other contra-indications for kiting. The kites and flying lines are excellent for grounding lightning so at the first flash of lightning or rumble of thunder get your kite down as fast as possible. Likewise, the kite that dumps itself in the electricity lines will not only fry itself and possibly the flyer, it will quite conceivably short out the power grid and could land you with a hefty fine from the electricity company. It goes without saying that sites next to roads and railways are a complete no-no and power kiting anywhere near an airport is usually prohibited.

Specific Safety Rules

All power kites worth spending the money on come with full operating instructions and a safety warning notice. Read them well before you take your kite out for the first time. There are some specific safety rules that apply to kiteboarding, buggying and the more extreme activities, which we'll cover in later chapters, but here is your general safety summary:

- **Never fly near overhead power lines, airports, roads or railways.**
- **Never fly in thunderstorms.**
- **Always select a safe launching and landing area away from people and obstacles.**
- **Always use appropriate safety equipment.**
- **Disable your kite and lines when not in use.**
- **Never allow inexperienced kite fliers to use your equipment.**

One final safety thought before you launch your power kiting career. With the exception of when you're using kites for getting airs, when it's recommended you hang on to the controls at all times, your ultimate safety mechanism is to let go of the control handles or bar completely if you feel that it's all getting to be too much. The kite will blow downwind and eventually come to ground without the retaining tension on the flying lines. But this really is a final solution and all other efforts should be made to control the kite first. It can present a potentially enormous danger to other kiters or bystanders and means there is a lot of sorting out of lines and kites to do before you can fly again. Never attempt to stop an escaped kite by grabbing the flying line as it may cut into your hand. In kiteboarding, where the biggest power is needed, safety systems and leashes are now commonplace so that you can let the kite go and recover it again without risk to yourself or others.

Wind

If you're just starting out with power kites or are just in it for a bit of recreational fun, a simplistic understanding about wind speeds may well be enough. Is there enough wind to fly or not? If there's enough, is there just enough to fly or is it strong enough to make flying good fun? It's a popular misconception that you need a roof-lifting wind to fly kites. Normally, most kites will fly well in 10mph or more of wind. If you're getting a bit more specialized and power kiting takes the form of getting in your buggy or out on your board as often as possible, then a little more detail will be needed. For instance, you'll almost certainly have alternative kite sizes for different wind strengths. In a light wind (10mph or 10 knots) you will need to fly a big kite (an 8 or 9 square meter ram air foil, for example) to achieve traction. The same kite in a big wind (20mph or 20 knots or more) will be an uncontrollable monster and you'll need less kite to achieve the same power – a 2, 3 or 4 square meter kite. It's the same principle as sailing and windsurfing. The more serious you get, the more kites you'll have, so that you can always maximize your fun whatever the wind.

All good kites come with recommended wind ranges for optimum performance, which you should take good account of. Flying outside these wind ranges might cause damage to your kite or yourself. A set of kites with overlapping wind ranges will cover you for every eventuality.

Measuring Wind Speed

Kite wind ranges are normally expressed in wind speeds. There are numerous different ways of measuring speed: Beaufort (force 1, 2, 3, and so on, as on the shipping forecast), miles per hour, kilometers per hour, knots, meters per second. Understanding these and what is the right range for your kite is one thing, actually measuring it on the day you're out flying is another altogether. There are a few ways

▲ *A wind meter*

of doing this. First, watch the weather forecast on television, where there is usually a forecast of wind speeds (in miles per hour, mph) in a circle on the chart, with a little arrow attached to show direction. A better and more accurate way would be to buy yourself a pocket wind meter but you'll need to spend a decent amount of money to get something at all accurate. If you're sailing from a center or club they normally have a high-quality anemometer on site giving a constant accurate reading. A less scientific but nonetheless useful method is to look for wind indicators in the environment – they can give you an enormous amount of information. Watch for smoke or clouds in the sky, flags and trees moving, look at the surface of water for rippling, white horses, waves, and so on. Study the table on page 21 which shows all the official measures and a list of indicators you can use.

With time you'll learn to "feel" the wind and make your decision on which kite to use from your experience. You'll know instinctively when to switch to a smaller or bigger kite from your muscle and brain memory of similar situations. One thing you do need to understand is that there's a point at which kiting becomes dangerous however you're doing it. Watch what the serious flyers and riders do. When it gets too big they stay indoors. As a rough guide, anything over Force 6 (30mph) is going to start making things very exciting to the point of danger and foolhardiness. Over Force 8 (40mph) and you've only got yourself to blame.

There are a couple of other factors to consider as well. Your flying lines can make a big difference to how the kite performs in different wind speeds. It's all a question of weight, diameter, stretch, the kind of activity you're doing, and the drag that results from that combination of factors. Modern power kite flying lines are made of materials that significantly reduce all three factors, but you may still be able tweak extra miles per hour of wind range out of your kite by flying on lighter or heavier lines – lighter to generate more power and fly faster, heavier to fly slower and "brake" the kite. All reputable power kite manufacturers suggest in their instructions the appropriate strength flying lines for average and heavy use. If in any doubt, consult your dealer or another expert; inappropriate line strength will either spoil your fun or present a risk to yourself and others.

Wind Direction

Wind direction may be a crucial factor if you're a kiteboarder, as an offshore wind (one that blows out to sea) can result in your being blown into the danger of the open sea. But the main thing to consider is the smoothness of the wind. Beach sites are great because often, with an onshore wind (one that blows in from the sea) or side wind, the wind is smooth and

| WIND SPEED | | | | | WIND-SPEED INDICATORS (PROBABLE) | |
Force	Mph	Knots	Kph	Meters per sec	Description	At Sea	On Land
0	<1	<1	<1	0–0.2	Calm	Smooth as glass	Calm; smoke rises vertically
1	1–3	1–3	1–5	0.3–1.5	Light Air	Ripples with no appearance of scales; no foam crests	Smoke drift indicates wind direction; vanes do not move
2	4–7	4–6	6–11	1.6–3.3	Light Breeze	Small wavelets; crests of glassy appearance	Wind felt on face; leaves rustle; vanes begin to move
3	8–12	7–10	12–19	3.4–5.4	Gentle Wind	Large wavelets; crests begin to break, scattered whitecaps	Leaves and small twigs in motion; light flags extended
4	13–18	11–16	20–29	5.5–7.9	Moderate Wind	1–4ft waves; numerous whitecaps	Leaves and loose paper raised up; flags flap; small branches move
5	19–24	17–21	30–38	8.0–10.7	Fresh Wind	4—8ft waves; many whitecaps; some spray	Small trees begin to sway; flags flap and ripple
6	25–31	22–27	39–50	10.8–13.8	Strong Wind	8–13ft waves forming white-caps everywhere; more spray	Large branches in motion; whistling heard in wires
7	32–38	28–33	51–61	13.9–17.1	Near Gale	13–20ft waves; white foam blown in streaks	Whole trees in motion; resistance felt in walking against wind
8	39–46	34–40	62–74	17.2–20.7	Gale	13–20ft waves; edges of crests beginning to break; foam in streaks	Whole trees in motion; resistance felt in walking against wind (again)
9	47–54	41–47	75–86	20.8–24.4	Strong Gale	20ft waves; sea begins to roll; dense streaks of foam	Slight structural damage occurs; shingles blow from roofs
10	55–63	48–55	87–101	24.5–28.4	Storm	20–30ft waves; white churning sea; rolling is heavy; reduced visibility	Trees broken/uprooted; considerable structural damage occurs

controlling the kite is much easier, as it behaves consistently. An offshore wind will have to come past the land mass and any other obstacles behind. It will be what kiters call lumpy. A lumpy, gusty wind will make the kite fly erratically and, depending on its size, dangerously. Many inland sites have lumpy wind for exactly this reason. To give you a guide, it usually takes the wind up to seven times the height of the obstacle in lateral distance to smooth itself out again (so a 100 foot tree or building will have a wind shadow up to 700 feet long). Find the most open, exposed site you can and position yourself as far downwind of any obstacles as possible.

The Wind Window

The wind window – or if you have come to power kiting from another wind sport you might be familiar with the term wind envelope – is the field of maneuver described by the kite on the end of its flying lines as it moves around the sky with the flyer standing still. It dictates how much and what type of power your wing will generate. Try for yourself: there's a limit to each side of you and

▶ *Kite in the parked position*

how far over your head that you can fly the kite before it either stops moving or loses power, stalls and falls out of the sky. With you as a fixed point at its center the wind window described resembles the surface of a quarter sphere. There really isn't any kite that can make the full quarter sphere requiring a full 180-degree lateral pass – the average is more likely to be 130 to 140 degrees. The illustration on page 23 will help you understand. Bear in mind that the wind, specially light wind, can shift and change direction. Your orientation shifts with the wind until you relocate the new window center and edges. On a beach site wind shift could well be associated with the tides and a flat calm day can easily turn into a real hoolie following a tide change.

Traditionally, sport and power kites are most efficient when they are at the center of the wind window, flying horizontally across the sky at roughly head height or slightly above. Here they move fastest and pull hardest. Keep flying horizontally and the kite will gradually slow down and lose power as it reaches the edge of its window. Turn the kite around and fly back across the wind window. As you reach the center turn upwards and fly the kite straight up the wind window. If the wind is strong enough you'll notice

" There are great starter or recreational kites on which you can learn the basic skills and add to them. Power kiting is really sociable and friends can join kites together for a bigger pull. **"**

ANDREYA WHARRY professional kiteboarder
and power kite instructor

3 Two-line Power Kites For Land Use

You could say that anyone who's not a board rider or buggy driver is a recreational flyer, just out for the pure fun and a few laughs, not too worried about developing their flying skills and not too concerned about getting onto a board or into a buggy. If you're the kind of person who likes to keep your kites in the car to use occasionally, when there's a good wind blowing, you're a recreational flyer. But if you like to get out as often as you can with the biggest rig possible that's appropriate for the conditions, with the added spice of big jumps, fast buggying or carving up the surf, then you're an altogether different beast.

Most people who try power kiting for the first time or start to fly regularly do indeed start on a regular, two-control line, ram air or air foil power kite. For many people the first step is going out with a friend who's already converted to kite power and having a go on their kite. The second step normally comes the day afterwards when you hunt down your nearest power kite dealer and buy yourself one because, like 99.9% of first-timers, you're an instant convert. If your ultimate aim is to take power kiting to its limits then it's certainly possible to learn kite skills on one of the big traction wings, but you can learn more, much more quickly, if you start with an exciting, sky-sweeping two-line power kite. On its 40-meter lines it really fills up the sky, moving fast and pulling hard, and few other kites are able to describe the shape and extent of the wind window as well as a good, basic, two-line power kite.

When you're ready you can switch to the slower-moving but heavier-pulling bigger kites – the serious "grunt" versions. The increase in pull through the wingspans is impressive and with a 3 or 4 square meter kite flying in 15mph of good steady wind you'll be getting one of the best workouts you've had in ages. Remember, smaller kites move faster and pull less, bigger kites pull more and move more slowly. A 3 square meter kite will give you a compromise of pull combined with fast flying speed, whereas a 4 square meter or bigger kite will be much less fun to actually fly but will deliver much more in terms of power. And even if you do progress to far more serious power kiting extremes, you'll still keep your old basic kites in your kite bag because – for pure fun and recreational flying – little can beat, for you, friends, or family, a good two-line power kite.

Descriptions And Uses

Time to get technical again and take a close look at these basic ram air kites or wings, see how they're built and what makes them tick.

The Flexifoil Stacker was the first and original modern power kite, created

◀ *A stack of 6-ft stackers*

> **Simplicity has helped it remain a popular recreational power kite but its efficiency and reliability, like all functioning designs, depends on a combination of good conception, suitable materials and quality workmanship.**
>
> **ANDREW JONES Flexifoil co-designer**

30 years ago. Although there have been changes of materials used, its construction today makes it basically the same kite as the original concept. What's more, it has inspired power kite design and manufacture all over the world. For a time during the early 1990s there were people trying to power kite with rigid-framed, steerable, delta-wing sport kites. But the raw power and unbeatable durability of ram air kites, specially under heavy crash impacts, meant that the ram air quickly became the overwhelmingly dominant power kite form.

That's why nowadays the power kite market, at least as far as dry land use is concerned, is dominated by ram air foils. There are plenty of good makes on the market and bigger US manufacturers such as New Tech, Premier, Prism, and Slingshot all have ranges of ram air power kites that fall into this category, as do overseas manufacturers such as Flexifoil and Invento. If your local dealer doesn't stock the brand you want, try mail order or internet shopping instead; it's a

competitive market and it won't take you long to find what you're looking for.

A ram air power kite is best described as a tethered aerofoil wing. It's similar in basic structure to a modern aerobatic parachute or paraglider. The kite is essentially two rectangular sheets of fabric held together lengthways and separated to give it a three-dimensional shape by a series of ribs between the two sheets. This three-dimensional shape is critical as it dictates the amount of lift or pull delivered. The ribs divide the kite wing into sections called cells. Another way of looking at it is to say that the wing consists of a series of cells joined together. The kite is sealed at the rear (trailing) edge but the front (leading) edge has open vents, sometimes with a gauze covering to allow the kite to inflate, which it does under wind pressure, and also to prevent detritus finding its way inside the kite where it could impede performance. Once inflated the kite has an aerofoil profile, that is to say, in cross section it is similar to a conventional airplane wing, fat at the front edge tapering to a point at the back. It's like an airplane wing and, just like an airplane wing, it's the difference in speed of airflow over the two surfaces of the wing leading to a corresponding difference in air pressure that generates the power and forward movement (or lift in the case of the plane).

Those of you who've had a look at a paraglider or a parachute will be familiar with the complex structure of "shroud" lines coming from points all over the underside surface of the wing. These usually join together at two points, one on each side of the wing, and these two points are what the pilot's harness attaches to, usually hanging a little way below on two extension lines. All that string and the need to keep it in good order can be a daunting prospect but it is essential to maintain the wings carefully as they have no frame and require a structure of shroud lines to maintain their shape in flight. Otherwise the kite collapses in on itself, becoming a flightless piece of cloth in the sky.

A completely soft aerofoil kite needs a similar structure and many ram air power kites are just like this. The Flexifoil concept avoided this issue by using a device that formed part of the patent it lodged to protect its invention and ensure

▶ *Close-up of ripstop Chikara*

its uniqueness. Instead of a complex shroud or "bridle" (in kitespeak) the kite has a single flexible rod that fits into a pocket that runs across the leading edge of the kite and keeps the sail spread out in the correct shape to fly. The rod also helps the kite self-adjust its angle of attack against the wind, pivoting around the spar in different areas of the wind window and under different degrees of power. The sail tips and the control lines are attached to the tips of this rod. Whether it's a Flexifoil type or a conventional ram air, once inflated and with the tension of the control lines fixed to you, the flyer, a power kite has an uncontrollable need to move forwards and it is up to you to pilot it around the sky.

Early on in the history of power kite construction, a fabric was identified that gave the kites the durability necessary for commercial success, one that is still in use today. Sail cloth nylon, as used on yachting sails, known as ripstop, was the obvious choice, having all the qualities required to complete the power kite formula: lightweight, tough, durable, and low stretch. Ripstop comes in many grades or weights and for kites the lightest one was selected: spinnaker nylon. In time kite industry demands were so great that fabric manufacturers began to make ripstop nylon specifically for kites. Almost

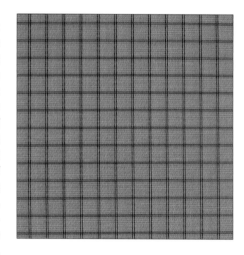

all modern power kites are now made from ripstop nylon, specially designed for kite manufacture. The excellent color ranges available mean that there's a good choice of kite colors, so power kites look great – an important consideration as, with any luck, you're going to spend a lot of time looking at them up in the sky.

There's another two-line power kite type that needs mentioning at this point, one that combines the features of delta and ram air technology in a simple design that is both a useful learning tool and can also deliver serious power. The NASA wing, as it is known nowadays, should more properly be described as the Rogallo wing in deference to its inventor, Frank Rogallo, an aeronautics engineer working for the National Aeronautics and Space Administration (NASA) in the 1940s and 50s. His invention was originally conceived as a kite at a time when there was relatively little interest in them. His idea was based on the principle of a flexible rather than fixed-form (framed) wing where the kite adapted its shape to the wind flow rather than the other way round. His patent, lodged in 1948, has provided the basis for all forms of delta wing design (for example, hang gliders, delta wing stunt kites, microlites) ever since. In fact it was NASA who saw the potential, not for using it as a kite, but rather as a type of parawing that could be deployed and controlled with great accuracy for the re-entry and landing of returned space capsules. With its central keel formed by the tension of its shroud or bridle lines, the two supporting wing areas generated the kite's form and then lift.

The modern NASA wing power kite is a completely soft kite flown on two or four lines, but instead of a double surface of kite with a volume in between that's filled by the wind, the NASA wing is a single sheet of sail cloth, cut and sewn in such a way that the volume and aero-

▶ *NASA wing*

© Invento GmbH

dynamic form is achieved by the kind of hollowing effect you'd see on a yachting spinnaker sail. NASA wings are available (or can be easily made) in varying sizes to deliver the power needed for your chosen activity in varying wind conditions. Although different in concept and construction, the NASA wing type of kite still performs in the same way up in the sky. It's a cheap and simple solution to the need to generate power but,

compared with today's sophisticated and specialized power kite designs, lacks sufficient mobility and control to make it the best option for most of the current popular power kite sports. But you can always tell anyone who says that "kite flying isn't exactly rocket science" that they're completely wrong.

As has been explained, to get more power, generally speaking you have to fly a bigger kite. Making the kite bigger means increasing the surface area that is exposed to the wind, adding to its span, and frequently its depth – "bolting on" extra cells to achieve the size required. This affects something called the aspect ratio – the ratio of the kite's depth to its span. Lower aspect ratio kites (more rounded or square) tend to be more stable, while higher aspect ratios (more elongated) are more efficient and powerful. Finding the perfect balance is the kite designer's skill. Frequently the depth and span are changed in rough proportion to each other so that the change of aspect ratio is not too great, and to give different-sized kites of the same model a similar feel in terms of general flying and handling.

There are exceptions to the "power increase through sail size increase" principle, such as the Flexifoil kite and the Prism Stylus. Although sold in differing sizes (as are other kites), their design makes it relatively simple to link or stack two or more kites together on the same control lines as a way of boosting your power. Kites of similar or different sizes can be mixed together to give an effect that is both muscle-stretching and eye-pleasing at the same time.

Flown singly or in stacks, a basic two-line power kite is ideal for learning how to handle kite power and can be used for taking your first steps in kite traction:

body dragging, getting airs, and so on. It's possible to use them for buggying but by no means as easy as if you use one of the kites designed specifically for that. Although we're talking about an adult toy, relatively young children – from age 10 upwards, depending on physique, manual dexterity, and so on – are perfectly capable of flying smaller power kites (kids often learn much faster than adults) but will need supervision in case the kite starts to pull too much. Saying that, with their sophisticated harnesses, de-power and safety systems to deal with the immense power of their specialized water-use kites, professional kiteboarders as young as 14 are not just entering but winning international kiteboarding competitions against adult riders. In 2003 a 9-year-old girl kiteboarder made her international tour debut, outscoring several of her adult competitors. In the correct circumstances there's absolutely no reason why children shouldn't enjoy the thrills of power kiting too. Don't be scared, but be very, very careful.

That applies to everyone, not just children. If you're thinking of getting into serious kite power, learning and completely learning how to fly basic power kites can be an important stage. You may quickly get bored with the simplicity of it but there may well be

times in the future when your understanding of how kites fly and the wind window in which they do so will give you a much more intuitive feel for them whichever discipline you're trying to do, maybe saving you crucial hundredths of a second to make a decision that could either endanger or preserve your life.

Set-up And Pack-up Procedure

When you buy your first quality power kite, it should come in some kind of storage bag, with an instruction manual, flying lines and controls, and in some cases a safety and kite maintenance manual. If any of these items are missing, contact the shop where you bought the product, or the manufacturer direct. You are thoroughly recommended to take the whole thing home, read the instruction manual, unpack, familiarize yourself with and re-pack your new toy at least once in the calm of your living room before you head off to your nearest flying site for a blast. Standing in a windy field trying to read the manual and control the flapping nylon sail at the same time is not conducive to happy power kiting. Reading the instructions, you'll become aware of how simple these kites are to prepare for action. A quick run-through confirms it. Follow the instructions and you can't really go wrong. And if you do manage to go wrong, take the kite back to your local dealer for some advice.

In practice out in the field or on the beach, you'll need to be able to immobilize the kite at this point by weighting down its trailing edge or upwind tip with sand or dirt. To do this the kite must be lying on its back, either perpendicular to the wind direction with the trailing edge upwind and the open vented leading edge downwind, or lengthways downwind with the trailing edge nearest the center of the wind window and the open vented leading edge facing towards the window edge. If you're unable to immobilize your kite for the set-up and launch phases, you'll need a helper to hold the kite and then give you an assisted launch (see later in this section).

With the kite fully prepared it's time to head back to your equipment bag for your flying (control) lines and handles or wrist straps. First, take the flying lines. There are two lines packed together on one line winder and they're ready to use with a sleeved loop on each end of each line. The quality of the lines you use can make a huge difference to the efficiency, response, and general flying of the kite. Nowadays all power kite manufacturers

recommend using a high-tech flying line such as Spectra (Dyneema) to get the best performance from your kite. Both are synthetic fibers. Spectra was developed as part of the American space exploration programme and Dyneema is a similar product made in Europe. Both these high-quality flying lines are strong, lightweight, low diameter, have less than 5% stretch and are very slippery. They enable kites to fly efficiently with minimal drag and once "flown in" (a few hours' flying pulls any remaining stretch out) give a "fly by wire" feel of immediate response. Conventional nylon or polyester lines are heavier, fatter and have up to 20% stretch. Many manufacturers recommend Spectra (Dyneema) line packs nowadays. Their slipperiness means you can fly easily with multiple twists in the lines but their chemical make-up gives them a low melting point and explains the need for a Dacron sleeve at each end, where the knots are tied.

There's no such thing as an industry standard for attaching flying lines. What has actually happened has been more a consensus of common sense but the result has been the same: almost without exception kite flying lines are attached to kites in the same way, whether you're in Albuquerque or Adelaide. With the kites pulling hard on your flying lines all

that's needed is a simple slip knot that will pull securely tight, with no risk of coming loose or undone on its own but which, miraculously, can be undone when desired, quickly and simply. Just such a knot exists, called the lark's head or lark's foot. It requires a loop at the end of one line from which the "lark's head" is formed, and a stopping knot at the end of the other line for the lark's head to grip against. Almost all power kites now come with stopping knot attachment points and flying line sets that have pre-formed loops on the ends. If you are at all confused about attaching your flying lines, go back to the dealer where you bought the kite, or contact the manufacturer if that's not possible. Incorrect line attachment could risk serious injury to yourself or a third party. Some manufacturers, specially those involved in kiteboarding, now provide color-coded line sets with co-ordinated handles or control bars precisely to avoid this risk.

To attach the kite: unwind a few meters of both lines, separate them and take one end to each of your kite's bridle points (see your kite instructions) or kite tip. Now make a lark's head knot in the looped end, as shown on in our step-by-step instructions on page 32 (this is the single most useful knot in power kiting so learn it now). Place the lark's head knot on the attachment toggle just behind the stopping knot and pull it tight up against the stopping knot, as shown in your instructions. Repeat for the other control line. And, yes, it really is as simple as that. Afterwards unwind the flying lines upwind away from the kite. Flexifoil kites have a different attachment system whereby you attach your lark's head knot to the single flexible rod that forms the leading edge – see the excellent Flexifoil instruction manual for full details.

Once you've unwound the lines you're ready for the control handles, wrist straps or bar. Often these will be pre-attached and your control lines measured to precise, equal lengths. If not, they usually attach with the same lark's head knot as before, although it might be achieved in a slightly different way depending on the make and model of kite you have. If the handle system has attachment toggles like the kite bridles, it's a simple repeat process of the lark's head knot, taking care that you correctly attach the left and right lines to their appropriate handle or tip of the control bar. Some wrist straps have a steel ring as their attachment point. In this case, take the looped end of your flying line and pass it through the metal ring on the end of the straps and then pull the strap through the line loop.

▶ How to make a lark's head knot

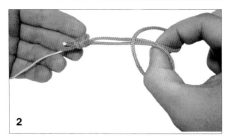

1

2

3

4

Pull it tight and the lark's head will form itself around the metal ring. The great thing about the lark's head is that it's a slip knot. The more you pull the tighter it locks so there's no chance of it coming undone in flight. But as soon as the tension is released (after landing the kite) it's relatively easy to pull loose and undo.

How To Launch, Fly And Land

Launching

Launching can be achieved with assistance or on your own: assisted launch to help you when you're learning, or for strong or gusty wind days; solo launch for normal circumstances. Here are the instructions for assisted launching:

■ **Position yourself so that the kite is downwind of you, slightly off to one side (the closer to the window edge the stronger the wind). Your flying lines are attached and untwisted with the appropriate line going to each hand. Adopt a good body position, hands in the handlebar position, just in front of your torso, arms slightly bent and elbows tucked in, knees slightly flexed ready for the kite to launch, and start pulling.**

■ Your helper should hold the kite from behind by the back surface, first of all lifting the leading edge or downwind tip (depending on how your kite is laid out) allowing the open vents to inflate the body of the kite with wind. As the kite reaches full inflation the helper must stay behind the kite, now holding only by the trailing edge or upwind tip.

■ When you're sure the kite's ready and there's enough wind, call to your helper to release the kite. The helper should not try to throw the kite into the air. The kite should fly out of the helper's hand, straight up the middle or edge of the wind window.

■ If you are launching from near the window edge you will need to steer the kite up the edge of the wind window until it reaches its hover point at the zenith. This is done by pulling back slightly on the control line nearest the center of the wind window until the kite reaches the center point, at which moment you bring your hands to the parallel "neutral" position. Be careful to steer the kite gently at first – steering too hard may result in bringing the kite directly into the power zone of the wind window before you're ready or able to deal with it.

■ In lighter wind the flyer may need to take a few steps backward at the moment of launch to help the kite up into stronger air currents. Avoid lifting your hands and arms

" **My advice to anyone starting out in power kiting: never ever underestimate the power of the wind and respect the elements to the full, keep the wind at your back and GO BIG!** "
JASON FURNESS Flexifoil team kiteboarder and tester

to encourage the kite to climb as this actually makes controlling the kite more difficult. Keep your elbows tucked into your sides ready to start steering.

We'll look at steering in a moment but first let's quickly run through solo launching.

There are two ways of doing this, requiring the kite to be set up and immobilized in one of the two positions described above in the set-up phase. Remember that in strong winds it can be dangerous to set up a (larger-sized) power kite for a straight-on launch in center window where it will power up hard and fast. Strong winds mean launching nearer the edge. Let's start with the best practice method, one you're well advised to learn if you're considering any of the more serious kite sports, which require dangerously large kites and good piloting skills. Here are the instructions for solo launching according to the best-practice method:

■ Make sure that the kite is lying on its back, lengthways downwind, leading edge facing the edge of the wind window.

■ Start by pulling gently on the line attached to the furthest (downwind) tip. As the tip lifts up the open vents will allow the kite sail to begin to inflate. Pull gently but steadily. The more you pull this line the more of the kite that will ride up and inflate. You will need to step backwards to maintain your body position and lift more of the kite off the ground.

■ The kite will rise up onto one tip, standing almost vertical. Keep the same amount of pull with your top hand but don't increase it. Instead you need to pull back equally on both lines to lift the kite off the ground fully. A few steps back may be needed for final lift-off.

■ Maintain your steering position to guide the kite up the edge of the wind window to the hover position at the zenith (in the center at the top of the window), at which point you can neutralize your steering (bring your hands parallel) again to keep the kite steady.

The second way is not recommended for bigger-sized kites in strong winds but is perfectly OK for small to medium-sized power kites in reasonable (moderate) winds. It's the other set-up we described, where you weight down the trailing edge, and can or should be done much closer to the center of the wind window for the smoothest launch. This is the most exciting way to launch because you take off straight into the power zone of the wind window, causing the kite to power up harder and accelerate faster. Here are the instructions for the other method of solo launching:

■ **Bend your legs and keep your hands comfortably in a handlebar position, parallel, just in front of and to the sides of your body.**
■ **Pull back gently but steadily with both lines equally, which will involve stepping back slightly. The leading edge of the kite will lift up and the open vents allow the wind to inflate the body of the kite. Learn to control this phase – the slower you pull back, the slower the kite will inflate and the more ready you'll be for the next step.**
■ **Walking a few paces further backwards, keeping your hands parallel so you're pulling equally with both lines. As the kite inflates and the leading edge lifts further off the ground the sand or dirt with which you've weighted down the trailing edge will all tumble off leaving the kite free...**
■ **...to launch itself, straight up the wind window towards the zenith. Be ready for the power to kick in, keep your hands parallel and elbows tucked in to keep the kite flying straight up the wind window, unless there are minor adjustments to make if the kite launches unevenly.**

Like anything, practice makes perfect, so persevere if you don't get it straight off. Once the kite is inflated you should follow the same procedure as for the assisted launch. Normally the kite should lift off on its own but you may need to help it up the first few feet. Don't jerk with your arms; pull back by walking steadily and smoothly backwards. Losing a few meters backwards is no problem as, all being well, you're going to be pulled forwards again once the kite is flying. If it doesn't launch fairly quickly, go and set it up and try again. Dragging the kite across the ground too much is a sure way to damage it. Use the assisted launch if needed.

For anyone using a Flexifoil power kite, there are some crucial differences to the launch technique (refer to your instruction manual for precise details). The differences apply to flyers and helpers and are important to understand. Once successfully launched, all differences end – like every other power kiter, now you're up and you're ready to fly!

Flying

If you can steer a bike or a car you can fly a power kite. The main thing is to keep your movements as smooth as possible and avoid steering jerkily. When you launch the kite it will fly straight up into the sky (if this doesn't happen, check the troubleshooting section that follows). You can either wait until it reaches a hover or parked position above your head to start steering it (you'll have to watch out that you don't over-fly and drop the kite out of the sky), or preferably take control of it before it reaches the top of the wind window, thereby keeping it moving – exactly what power kites like best. Remember that the stronger the wind the quicker the kite flies and the faster your reactions will need to be. Try in a moderate wind first unless or until you're feeling really confident. These are the basic movements:

■ **As the kite reaches three-quarters of the way up the wind window, pull back a short distance, smoothly and firmly on the right line. The kite flies to the right.**
■ **Pull similarly on the left line. The kite flies to the left.**
■ **Bring your hands parallel and the kite flies straight up the wind window to a hover (the zenith position).**

You can spend a bit of time moving backwards and forwards across the sky like that if you like, but it's more interesting to start doing some loops:

- Pull on the right line, this time keeping the pull going so that the kite flies to the right and then describes a circle downwards to the right. Don't pull the kite into a really tight spin as this tends to "stall" the kite or make it fold in on itself. A wider, smooth loop is good, enough to bring the kite around in a complete loop, the bottom of which should be a good few yards above the ground. A combined pull with the right and push with the left, just like on a bike, makes the smoothest turn. Keep pulling on the right line until the kite comes around and is pointing straight up the window again.
- As the kite comes around full circle and is pointing straight up the wind window, bring your hands parallel with each other and it will fly straight up.
- At this point your lines are twisted around each other but don't worry, it makes almost no difference to the controls of the kite. Don't cross your hands to compensate. To untwist the lines all you need to do is pull on the left line hard and long enough to bring the kite around in a

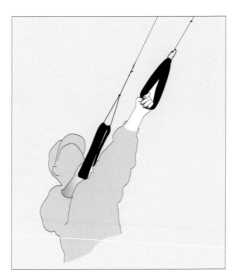

► Top: Right turn
► Bottom: Left turn

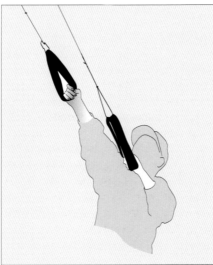

complete loop to the left at the end of which, if you bring your hands together in parallel, it should be once again pointing straight up the wind window, roughly in the center.
- As the kite comes up the wind window again it's up to you: right or left, and so on.

From this point on, the freedom of the sky is yours. You can start to play with wider and tighter loops and spins, explore the wind window and get to grips with the big lateral pull low down. The best bet to begin with is to keep flying right and left loops, a figure of eight on its side, which gives you a nice continuous pattern you can fly while you fully familiarize yourself with how the kite handles. You can fly quite a few loops in one direction before you need to untwist, which you will need to do at some point. Try to keep a rough count in your head and untwist from time to time.

Most power kites are very, very durable, which is just as well because almost certainly you'll have some big wipe-outs to begin with, crashing the kites hard into the ground. It's a big laugh, specially when someone else does it, but try and keep your crashes to a minimum, as repeated "unintentional ground contacts" will surely damage the kite eventually.

One other maneuver you will certainly want to try is a horizontal pass or sweep,

35

which with practice you'll be able to make closer and closer to the ground. Let's start with a right-to-left sweep:

- Pull on the right line as if to do a big right loop taking the kite down to the bottom quarter of the wind window.
- Now it's all a question of timing and may take a few tries to get it right. Instead of completing the loop, when the kite is pointing across the wind window bring your hands almost parallel, right hand slightly above the left, and fly the kite across the wind window from right to left.
- As the kite starts to slow down on the left side of the window, pull again on your right line so the kite turns until it's pointing across the window, going back the way it came. Bring your hands almost parallel again, but with the left above the right, and fly a pass back the other way.

Simply reverse the above, swapping left for right to fly it in the opposite direction. Soon you'll be confident enough to try those impressive ground-skimming passes, always watching out for other fliers and stray passers-by of course.

▶ *Leaning back against the pull, powering up with the kite in a right hand loop*

Landing

Sooner or later you're going to get tired, especially if you're flying a larger-sized kite, and want to land the kite or pass it on to someone else. In the latter case it's very simple. Fly your kite up to top center of the window, the park position, slip your wrists out of the straps and pass them quickly over to the next flyer. But, even so, sooner or later you'll still need to land. Do not fly a fully inflated and powered-up kite straight into the ground as it may well burst an internal cell or the sail itself. There's a safe and simple way to do it:

- Put the kite into a horizontal pass as described, low down if you can (but that will come with practice).
- As the kite passes center window and starts flying towards the edge, keep it going in that direction.
- The further the kite goes the more it slows down and the pull reduces until eventually the kite flies out of the wind window and falls gently to the ground. You can take a step or two forwards to make sure it settles on the ground if you like.

The kite will normally land upside down, lying on its back. Although it can't take off from that position you should still immobilize it immediately. If it's not upside down, go and put it that way. If you're just landing for a rest, a very good idea is to use a ground stake or peg for your straps. That way your kites can't blow away in a big gust and it will help keep your flying lines in good order. Most good kite shops sell ground stakes but in a pinch a big tent peg will do the trick. A non-abrasive weighted item such as a carry bag or water bottle makes a good kite weight

Congratulations, you're now an accomplished power kite flyer. Practice your controls to left and right until you're confident on both sides and you'll soon be ready to graduate to the serious stuff. That could be flying big stacks or moving onto the big traction wings for buggying and kiteboarding. Either way, you'll be joining very good company as one of the many millions of satisfied power kite owners.

Troubleshooting

Generally speaking, there's very little that can go wrong with a power kite. Nevertheless, you may find that your kite doesn't seem to be flying properly, in which case try checking the following instructions.

Landing the kite

If the power kite flies continually to one side:

■ **Check that both lines are the same length. The best way to do this is to peg the loops at one end to the ground and pull them tight from the other. A quick visual check will tell you. If they're unequal you will need to make an adjustment. Undo the loop of the longest line and undo the knots holding the line sleeving in place. Slide the sleeving along until it is equal with the shorter line, and retie the knots.**

■ **Check that you and the kite are positioned in the center of the wind window before launching. If the kite is near the edge it will want to fly towards the center as soon as it launches.**

If the power kite "bounces" violently in flight after launching:

■ **There may be sand or water inside the cells. Land the kite and try to remove the sand through the vents.**

■ **The sail may be very wet. Dry the sail thoroughly before attempting to re-launch.**

If the wingtips flap during flight:

■ **The fabric may be worn or damaged. The more it flaps the more it will damage the fabric weave and the coating.**

▶ Top: Spectra flying lines
▶ Bottom: Damaged kite

If you've tried those solutions and the kite still won't perform, go straight back to your dealer or contact the manufacturer directly. It could be a result of faulty manufacture but it could equally be a simple mistake you're making.

The kites are guaranteed against faulty manufacture but not against faulty flying. Kites may well end up getting damaged, so many dealers and manufacturers run a repair service, which you can use via your dealer or direct. Small hole repairs can be made yourself with a repair kit. Larger tears should be sent away for repair immediately. Check your kites over regularly and get repairs done quickly. Running without a repair is inviting bigger trouble later and may risk your own personal safety. And you'll have to face the fact that if you really hammer your kite, flying day-in day-out for long periods, specially in bright sunlight with its harmful ultra-violet, it (the sail fabric primarily) is going to wear out completely one day.

Stacking

Stacking is the most common term given to the linking together and simultaneous flying of two or more stunt, sport or power kites on one set of control lines (also known as flying "in train"). Flexifoils are virtually unique in that they can be easily stacked together. This is not strictly the case as it is possible to stack other makes of power kite, notably Prism's Stylus, but the Flexifoil design makes it very simple where other, completely soft kites are usually a much more difficult proposition. Different sizes of kite can be stacked together, although it works better with equal-sized kites. If you do decide to stack different sizes, put the smallest kite at the front (nearest the flyer) for the best performance.

There are two main reasons for wanting to stack kites. The first reason is that by adding to the first kite you are increasing the pull on the end of your lines and hence the range of stuff you can do with the resulting traction. There's a rough formula for working out by how much you increase pull, assuming you're using same-sized kites. When you add a second kite you virtually double the pull. Adding a third adds half as much pull as the first two. A fourth will add about one-third of that, and so on. The point is that the pull increases to the extent that, should you decide for some reason to want to fly a stack of 208 Stackers (as Flexifoil did at the Le Touquet kite festival in 1993), you'll need three bulldozers to anchor the stack and three people heaving on each

▶ *6-, 8- and 10-foot Flexifoils stacked together*

line to turn it round in the sky. One advantage of stacking is that you can get together with a few mates and soon have some serious traction going. You'll need friends anyway because when you're flying big stacks in a decent wind you soon get tired and you can pass the stack on to someone else while you laugh at them being dragged all over the field.

Power kite pull is almost impossible to quantify in terms of things like pounds per square inch or barr, specially with the wind being such a variable factor. What is relatively clear is that you can roughly gauge how the kites pull in relation to each other, even in stacks. What is glaringly obvious is that building a big stack has the effect of radically increasing the power, so you'll need stronger flying lines and an even more heightened sense of your own and other people's safety.

The other main reason for stacking is that it looks brilliant – that goes for the flyer and anyone watching. With half a dozen kites stacked you've got a big and colorful object sweeping majestically around the sky. Looking at your kites, feeling the pull and power, and knowing that you are in control, is an immensely satisfying experience, specially if you know that at any moment you could switch that power to the maximum for some extremely radical fun. Flexifoil kites

have easy-to-follow instructions for stacking kites together in the instruction manual. There are two ways suggested and either will do the trick very nicely.

Whatever kite you try to stack, accuracy of measurement of the lines linking the kites (the stacking lines) is all important as any slight differences in stacking lengths will result in the stack not flying correctly, if at all. And there's a formula for the correct distance between stacked kites: roughly two-thirds of the length of the leading edge. With a non-Flexifoil type soft ram air power kite you will need to create attachment points on the rear of each kite in order to be able to add another behind. This is not as simple as it sounds and the best method involves unstitching one of the kite ribs to stitch in place an attachment toggle on the rear face to attach the rear kite to. As I said, all very complicated (less so for a NASA wing type with its single sail surface), and that's before you've even made up your stacking lines to see if the two or more kites will actually work together. So if you really are intent on stacking then the simplest option is to go the Flexifoil way.

With additional kites attached you're ready to launch your stack, for which you'll almost certainly need a helper. Set up near the window edge with the kites lying lengthways downwind. Pull back on the line connected to the downwind tips to help them inflate while your helper holds the rear of the rearmost kite in the stack to steady them as they inflate. The kites normally inflate and lift off themselves but you may need to take some smooth, steady steps back to get them up. Do not jerk with your arms and don't drag the kites if they don't launch right away.

In flight, the stack should, if all your setting up and measuring is correct, lock into position. If it doesn't and the kites are always "shuffling" or simply not flying, there are a few things you can check:

- **Make sure all the kites are attached the right way up.**
- **Check that the stacking lines or loops are measured accurately.**
- **Try moving a problem kite to a different position in the stack.**

Whichever way you decide to build your stack you will need to check your stacking lines (and indeed your flying lines) regularly for wear and tear. The force and friction generated is considerable. Replace any that are worn or damaged right away.

When the stack is flying smoothly you will immediately feel the extra power and notice that the stack flies slower than a single kite. The more kites you add, the slower the stack flies and the stronger it pulls. It's very important that you are aware of the strength and maximum load of your flying lines. The recommended strength for a single kite will normally be sufficient for a stack of two kites the same size. Any more than that and you will need to get some stronger lines or risk a line breaking just when you didn't want it to, heavily powered up and getting into a skid or jump. The extra lifting power of the stack will more than compensate for any extra weight of the lines. Consult your local dealer or the kite manufacturer, who will be happy to advise you. Then you're ready for some more serious power kite action. For starters, how about a bit of skidding and getting some airs?

Skidding

Skidding or skudding is perhaps better described as body dragging and is often the first way most people discover the hidden joys of power kiting. Even if eventually you're heading for a kiteboard and the wide blue yonder, you've got to learn how to fly kites and you're going to learn skidding as part of your basic training. Skidding and getting airs (next section) require even more flying space, so make sure you've got plenty of clear space downwind of where you're flying, free of people and obstacles, to allow movement forwards.

The general idea is to generate enough consistent pull from the stack to pull you along, usually on your feet or on your back although you can try body surfing in shallow water on your front. You'll be aware that if you keep flying big figure eights with your kite(s) they gain and lose power in relation to their position in the wind window. What you'll need to do to go skidding any distance is keep the kites powered up for long enough to move you along. Here's how it goes:

- Steer the kites up the center of the wind window and begin a right-hand loop. You can try it in the opposite direction by substituting left for right if you like.
- As the kites come around their loop towards the center of the wind window they will begin to seriously power up. Get your feet flat on the ground and lean back to resist being pulled over on your front. You should feel yourself starting to move forward.
- Keep your shoulders back and your body in a straight line if possible, leaning backwards, shoulders behind hips behind feet. As the kite hits center window about halfway up, pull it into a tighter loop to keep it turning in the center window,

thereby keeping it fully powered up. Too tight a spin will lose power, so you may need a few practice runs to get it just right. Keep your body position and try to go with the kite, releasing the grip of your feet slightly until you're accelerating forwards.
- After a few turns of the kite you will need to reverse the direction of turn to untwist your lines but you'll want to keep the power on. Keep the kites roughly in center window and keep leaning back and sliding forward on the flats of your feet or back.
- You can "switch the power off" at almost any time by flying the kites upwards, out of center window (or out to one edge). Fly the kites up to the park position, stand up and walk back to your start point to have another go.

Beaches are great for skidding: hard, flat sand for speed, soft sand for really digging the feet in and "skiing" along. Inland sites are OK too but you'll have a bumpier ride. From personal experience I can thoroughly recommend a grassy playing field, recent rain and plastic waterproof trousers for one of the fastest skids you can get. Make sure you're properly decked out wherever you're going to fly. Decent ankle-supporting footwear, sweat shirt and pants to prevent scratching or grazing on the ground, even a crash

helmet, wrist guards and knee pads may be necessary, depending on the conditions and the size of your stack. With practice you'll be able to pull some amazing skids and have skid mark competitions with your friends – the longest skid wins.

Getting Airs

Otherwise known as kite jumping or moon-walking, getting airs is where power kiting really departs from normal ground-based kiting and turns into an exercise in anti-gravity and weightlessness. You may have seen other people getting air, down at your local beach or flying field or on some power kiting or extreme-sport video down at your local store. You may well have experienced kite jumping inadvertently during your flying and skidding stage but either way there's probably going to come a time when you want to see what it's like to get airborne kite-style. Kite jumping is not recommended, even by power kite manufacturers, and certainly not by us. But we do recognize that boys will be boys...

The first thing to say is that you cannot use kites to fly in the same way as a parachute (descending) or paraglider (descending or ascending) so please don't try. Nevertheless, now you really are going to

> " The first jumps I started doing were a real buzz, as with most people the first wasn't intentional! A little bit of knowledge is dangerous and you keep pushing things until Mother Nature kicks you where it hurts. "

ANDREYA WHARRY Flexifoil team kiteboarder and power kite instructor

have to think about some personal protection. The boots, helmets, and pads are much more necessary. There are many stories, including one about someone in Britain "flying" a river estuary, of jumpers picking up a secondary gust once up in the air ending up in a vastly different jump from the one they'd envisaged a few seconds before. Kite jumping can be a real ankle and wrist snapper with all those heavy landings, specially in the learning phase. Expect the unexpected and, above all, show proper respect for what you're doing. Even small jumps need big power and if things go wrong under those circumstances you could end up in serious difficulty.

It seems obvious that, when you jump, what you're looking for is lift rather than lateral pull. In fact a basic maxim is to concentrate on getting altitude and the wind speed will take care of distance. So you mustn't bring the kites too low down in the wind window or you'll simply end

◀ *Skidding*

up going for a facial scrape down the field. The kites must stay higher in the window, so you never use their full power. That's why you need a lot more kite up in the sky to get you airborne and that's why it becomes that bit more dangerous.

The ideal kite for getting airs will have fast acceleration to haul you up in the air and will be a two-line kite to reduce its maneuverability. If you use a four-line power kite (see Chapter 4 on quad-line power kites) you will need to be very careful as their extra maneuverability and strong acceleration are harder to control because of the brake line effect. Single large traction kites specifically designed for jumping, or stacks of smaller kites, are the best option. Whichever you use, you will be dealing with a huge amount of kite power.

You will need to resist the kites' pull for as long as possible until the moment of release, levering against them as the power builds up for the jump. On a beach you can even dig a hole to give you a wall to lever against. When the moment comes and you let go for your jump, everything happens very quickly and there's a lot of energy involved – your own and that of the kites. Jumping with 8 to 10 meters of sail in a 20mph wind means there's about 3 Gs of force on your body as you leave the ground. You're going to need to be reasonably fit and not easily breakable. It's probably not a good idea to start off at that level. Start small and work your way up. It won't be long before you're counting the seconds of flight and measuring your jumps in tens of meters. Discretion is very much the better part of valor in power kiting, however, and you shouldn't be embarrassed about stopping if conditions and the size or height of the jumps get to be too much. Alcohol's not the only pursuit where one too many can have fatal consequences.

These are the key instructions for getting airs:

■ Steer the kite(s) up to the park position at the top center or zenith of the wind window. Get ready to brace your body and find a good "lever" position. Without pulling the kite into a full loop, steer it across and down one edge of the wind window until it's about halfway up or down the wind window, pointing slightly towards

▶ *A jumper with a stack of Super 10's*

the edge. This is done with a slight pull on either the right or left line depending on which side you want to maneuver on. It's common to feel more confident setting a jump up from one side than the other, so try both and see which feels best.

■ Now pull slightly with the opposite hand to point the kite in towards the window center. It will accelerate increasingly fast and pick up power very quickly. Keep leaning back and levering with your body. In lighter winds you may find that running in the opposite direction to that which the kites are moving will help increase the power.

■ As the kites approach center window, roughly halfway up, steer them so they fly straight up the wind window. Keep your hands in neutral from this point; if you turn the kite back into the power zone you will land fast and hard – a real ankle job. At the same time you can release your resistance to the kite and will feel yourself pulled, jerked off the ground arms first, up into the sky, legs trailing behind you. Hold on tight and enjoy the weightless moment.

■ Watch the ground as it rushes up to meet you for touch down and swing your feet and legs forward pendulum style so you can land on your feet or back.

■ Once you've hit the ground again you can recover control of the kite. It should be flying up near the top of the wind window with little pull.

■ Pick yourself up and, keeping the kite up at the zenith, you can go back for another go. Either that or try and crawl to your cell phone to call an ambulance.

There's another way of generating lift that doesn't require levering against the kites' pull, the same maneuver described above for light winds. As you bring the kite across the window to initiate the jump, run in the opposite direction from the kite's direction of travel, remembering to steer it up the window at the appropriate moment. This creates the leverage and whips you up into the air as the kite powers up and drives up the wind window.

Make sure you're really confident before you try and hit any really big airs and it's unlikely you'll ever need that ambulance. Beaches are definitely a good bet, especially soft sand, as this affords a comparatively soft landing. Even so the landings can be heavy. If you do feel that it's all getting a bit too big or you pick up one of those second surges from a gust of wind, the best advice is not to let go, hang onto your wrist straps, and wait for the kites to bring you down again. The only circumstances in which this does not apply are when the kites are dragging or flying you towards a fixed obstacle such as a post, pier, wall, rock, or tree. Take a kite or two off your stack and try again, or wait for the wind to drop a little.

Power kiting really progressed with the introduction of soft ram air four-line kites. These easy-to-use high performance kite engines gave everyone a chance to get into kite traction sports on land, snow or water.

RAY MERRY owner of Cobra Kites, original Flexifoil co-designer

The Four-line Concept

As the face of power kiting has changed and all manner of extra traction possibilities have been opened up by harnessing kite power to include buggies, mountainboards and of course kiteboarding boards, so the performance requirements for power and traction kites have changed too. The easy-to-use standard power kite (or stack), though good enough to get you going for, say, buggying, wasn't specifically designed for the job and so it was no surprise that designers decided to put a clean sheet of paper on the drawing board when the time came to deal with the traction challenges. One important issue was the re-launching of the kite, not at all easy with a stack when you're sitting in a buggy or balancing on a board. Responding to an entirely different set of demands, power kite designers made a giant evolutionary leap to start developing vastly more sophisticated soft, frameless (no spars or stiffeners) airfoil traction kites, designed to meet the varied needs and usage options in the new power kiting disciplines.

Soft two-line power kites already existed, notably the Peel, designed by traction kiting pioneer, New Zealander Peter Lynn. These were generally slower-moving than Flexifoils, but could be made in big enough sizes to deliver the necessary "grunt" for buggying and the curious buggy-boat that Lynn was also manufacturing at the time, without the need for stacking. It was clear too from paraglider and parachute design that this type of wing could deliver big power. But there was to be another element to the change in format, one that has ultimately done much to facilitate the vast and rapid expansion of appeal in traction kiting.

During the late 1980s, the American kite manufacturer, Revolution, successfully developed their synonymous and truly revolutionary carbon fiber-framed, four-line sport kite, the Revolution #1. Instead of two control lines, the new kite had four, two each attached to left and right sides of the kite sail, one at the top and one at the bottom. Special control handles were made with two attachment points on each, one handle controlling each side of the kite. Whereas a two-line kite has its angle of attack (the angle of the sail against the wind) fixed to move the kite forwards all the time, with the new concept it was possible to engage forward movement by applying pressure to the top lines, then apply pressure to the bottom ones, thereby altering the angle of attack so that backwards became forwards, and one could slow the kite, stop it and move it in reverse. In fact, four lines technically gives 360-degree maneuverability. It was a curious combination of the kite's ultra-precise maneuverability and its ability to stand still that caught the eye. Traction kite designers quickly saw the possibilities and adapted the principle to soft traction foils. It was an enormous success and marked the point at which the numbers of people

▶ *Peter Lynn Rebble: Complex bridle and 4 control lines*

getting into power kites reached critical mass and the whole market became self-promoting and sustaining.

Lacking a frame, completely soft ram air kites need a multiple suspension point bridle system to hold their shape. But by adding two more control-line attachment or bridle points, and re-balancing the whole structure, the flyer can control the angle of attack of the kite more, using the control handles, and so create and use a different kind of lift. The four control lines make that control very sensitive and accurate.

There are always exceptions to the rule. Traction master Peter Lynn devised a kind of hybrid power kite concept, which he called the C-Quad. As the name would imply, it's a four-line kite, but not as we know it. It's a single skin kite (as opposed to double skin ram air), with volume cut into the sail panels, direct flying line attachment to the frame of the kite (comprising a leading edge arch and series of vertical battens), thereby avoiding the need for a complex bridle. It combines characteristics of delta and ram air technology and behaves in much the same way as a conventional ram air four line, delivering considerable power at

▶ *Four-line control handles with safety leash*
▶ *Four-line control handles – the brake position*

the cost of slightly less finesse of control. It's a kite that's suitable for land use and has seen considerable service on the water in its time. Less so nowadays, with the huge amount of more sophisticated equipment available, Peter Lynn kites included.

As it applies to power kites, even in the four-line scenario most of the work in terms of load bearing and steering control is effected with the front lines (this is not the case if flying from a control bar or flying an inflatable water kite, where the steering is mostly done by the rear lines). The rear lines are there most of the time to help keep the kite in the right shape and for "braking" it to reduce power. They are used much less for going backwards, other than for landing and for re-launching from the otherwise impossible face-down position. For this reason, generally speaking the front lines are stronger than the rear ones. The control handles are each in the form of a short bar, slightly curved near the top. Top and bottom on left and right sides of the kite connect to the corresponding top and bottom of each handle. There is a risk of attaching your flying lines upside down and nowadays many kites and line sets are sold with color-coded sleeved loops so you can tell at a glance which is which. Please take care when attaching your four control

lines that they are correctly attached, as incorrect attachment can render the kite uncontrollable and dangerous. Flying or steering the kite is achieved in very much the same way as before, pulling or pushing with left and right hands but retaining pressure on all four lines to keep the kite in shape. To brake the kite you gradually apply more pressure with the rear lines until the kite slows down to a complete stop and will eventually start moving slowly backwards.

The size and efficiency of these traction kites explains the increasing use of body harnesses (like those used by windsurfers) by serious power kiters. A loop of heavy line connecting the handles is hooked into the harness which enables you to carry most of the pull on your legs and body, relieving pressure on your arms (kiteboarder control bars have purpose-made harness loops). Steering happens as normal, with the loop of line sliding through your harness hook or pulley. You shouldn't consider using a harness until you have fully learned to fly your kite ordinarily. It doesn't take long to adapt to flying with four lines but you certainly should spend some time, as ever, fully familiarizing yourself with the flying controls of a smaller kite before you get radically powered up.

There's been a long-standing and false perception of kiting as an activity whose potential is limited by the flying line spaghetti scenario. The idea of four control lines can be quite intimidating in theory but in practice everything is geared towards simplicity. No one wants to waste their time untangling big line messes, and nowadays all aspects of power kiting are consumer-driven, geared to delivering maximum fun with minimum fuss. Kiting has sorted out its spaghetti issues and you needn't worry. You shouldn't have problems if you are organized about how you handle your flying lines. In any event they are a critical element of the whole kit and need to be respected as much as the kite itself. Always allow time at the end of your session to pack up in an orderly way, and always immobilize your kite and control handles properly when not in use. Bad winding and a kite that blows away down the field are two common causes of fouled lines.

One issue with all soft aerofoils, two or four line, is that they are very difficult (to the point of virtually impossible) to stack as we described in the section in Chapter 3 on stacking. It requires a different approach and is not just about having more or less power on the end of your control lines. An early idea from one UK manufacturer was a ram air kite wing with extra sections that could be quickly zip-fastened on or taken off. But the idea that got the majority vote was to have a range of kites in different sizes that would enable flying in a wide variety of winds. This is a similar principle to sail boats, windsurfers, and so on, who use their smallest sails in the biggest winds and vice versa. In most other respects four-line kites are no different, with the same wind window and other physical limits as their two-line predecessors. Some can still be adapted for flying on a two-line set-up – check with your dealer at time of purchase.

Just because a kite is soft, don't kid yourself that it cannot do serious damage or be seriously damaged. With no other visible means of support (a spar or frame), they are more susceptible and sensitive to nicks and tears in the fabric from ground contact. Overstretching can also be a problem, specially if a kite is flown at the limit or just above its recommended wind range for lengthy periods – not uncommon when a serious buggyer or kiteboarder is heavily powered-up, going for maximum speed or lift. And a heavy, vent-down, fully inflated and powered-up landing can easily burst a panel or, worse, one of the internal ribs that are critical to the airflow and pressure within the sail. Likewise, with so much power in play, slamming the kite or flying lines into innocent bystanders could cause them serious injury. Remember, safety is the responsibility of the flyer.

Since the development of soft, aerofoil or ram air power kite wings there's been a quantum leap in the number of power kite manufacturers who've come into the market to satisfy the increasing demand. There are strong arguments that competition is good for any market, stimulating technical advances and product design, all of which can only benefit the consumer. That's certainly true in this increasingly specialized market where the last ten years have been the most productive for the entire industry. There's already been growth, decline, and fall-out, and re-establishment of some kind of consistency in the short history of power kite manufacture. Those players in the market now generally have at least two complete ranges of four-line aerofoil or ram air kite wings, each designed to meet specific needs in the diverse and rapidly evolving demands of modern traction kiting. Generally speaking these will fall into two categories: one range suitable for entry level pilots but also able to help you progress; another range for experienced pilots looking for higher, competition-standard power and performance.

▶ *Ballistic: A low aspect ratio starter kite*

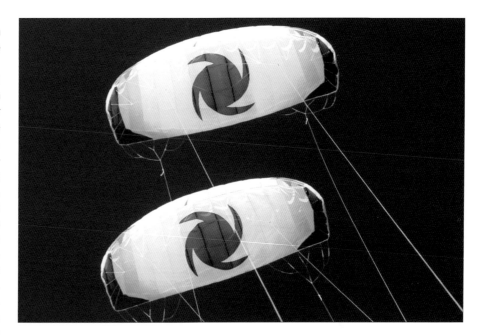

Quad-line Power Kites

Soft kites have no rods or frame to stiffen them. They inflate with wind pressure through a series of vents at the front and are held in shape by a complex bridle structure with multiple suspension points as described earlier. The extra controllability of the four-line set-up has made it possible for many more people to enjoy the kite buggy experience with far greater ease, allowing themselves to be pulled along and concentrating more on steering the buggy or landboard, less on piloting these super stable four-line kites. Not surprisingly four-line kites have quickly replaced the generally faster-moving two-line foils that had been the option previously.

One of the first big four-line soft kite successes, the Skytiger, was designed and developed in the early 1990s by original Flexifoil partner, Ray Merry, under the banner of his new Cobra Kites venture in America. This was quickly joined by the Quadrifoil brand, developed by American designer Robert Graham. Despite this

> " I don't believe in trainer kites. It's the flyer not the kite that needs to learn. I'm a cruiser and these kites take me everywhere I want to go, all over the beach, stable, solid and smooth. "
>
> COREY JENSEN WindPower Sports – Las Vegas, hard-core buggy pilot

early advantage, nowadays much of the US traction kite product, at least at a serious level, remains European with makes such as Advance, Flexifoil, JoJo, and Ozone available, but you'd have to add in the Peter Lynn range from New Zealand. Curiously, there's now a reverse move by inflatable kite manufacturers into the manufacture of ram air kites, fueled by the need for some kind of training kite for would-be kiteboarders and a sudden growth in popularity of snow kiting. That explains why companies such as North Kites and Slingshot, from a hardcore kiteboarding background, now have some quality ram air kites in their product ranges. Kiteboarding has also brought the possibility of effective de-power systems and quick releases much closer to the other power kiting disciplines because of the very essential nature of those things for the future of kiteboarding as a sport. Skytigers and Quadrifoils are still available,

although now they've been joined by all these other hugely versatile and successful four-line performers, but their place in traction kiting history is assured.

Beginner Quad Lines

A typical modern beginner four-line buggy kite will have an ultra-stable aerofoil, medium-aspect ratio, and be semi-elliptical in shape to minimize drag and increase its power-to-size ratio. There will be a series of vents, possibly with a gauze strip

across, running along the leading edge of the kite to allow it to inflate quickly for launch or re-launch, and to allow you to shake sand or other unwanted detritus out. There will be a multiple bridle or suspension-line structure, to keep the kite in shape, nowadays often made from tough-sleeved Dyneema. These kites are powerful but still easy to handle. They'll normally be available in a range of sizes from around 2 to 5 square meter; the smaller sizes are good beginner traction kites but the larger sizes require at least intermediate skill level because, despite their stable handling, they can nevertheless develop serious amounts of grunt!

This type of kite can be fantastically versatile, a great all-rounder and suitable for all land-based power kite activities such as they exist today: recreational flying, buggying, landboarding, blading,

> " Racing kites make me work harder and pay more attention in my buggy. Plenty of grunt and higher speeds when I want to max things out. "
>
> COREY JENSEN WindPower Sports – Las Vegas, hard-core buggy pilot

> " Nothing takes you higher faster than a top-end ram air. It's like a rocket launcher. If you want big airs and high adrenaline get one of these. "
>
> CHRIS CALTHROP pro kiteboarder

▶ *Crusing or racing a quad line kite is the ultimate kite buggy 'engine'.*

and snow kiting. What they are not designed for is water use: you should not, under any circumstances, try to use these types of power kite on water. They weren't designed for it and, anyway, there are other toys in the cupboard much better suited to that kind of thing.

High-performance Quad-lines

The latest twist in the power kite tale has taken kites onto the water and snow with the successful invention and popularizing of kiteboarding and snow kiting. Like windsurfing, but using a kite for power instead of a fixed mast and sail, kiteboarding has brought its particular set of requirements to bear on the creative forces behind modern kite design. For many of the pioneering kiteboard manu-facturers, the first solution to the kite for water or board use was to use an already-established Formula One model in their ram air foil range. Generally speaking these were performing at the top end of competition-buggying, high-performance ram airs. An early water pioneer was American Troy Navarro who competed at the X-Games in the early 1990s using

▶ *High altitude action with Ozone 'Frenzy' kite*

Merry's Skytiger kites (now considered low performance) on water. It was possible, but they were hardly the ideal tools for the job.

The pressure was on for manufacturers, and the responses came quickly. One of the first ram air kites to make a successful transition from land to water was the Blade, another Andrew Jones or Flexifoil original design. So successful was it that it's still available, now in its third generation of development as a frameless aerofoil kite with a multiple bridle and a high aspect ratio. Other designers and manufacturers have followed suit and, in the last few years, ever-more sophisticated ram air kites have been made. We'll deal specifically with kiting on the water later in the book; for now we're concentrating on using this type of kite on land.

A typical high-performance quad line kite has a particularly ellipsoidal, elongated outline with rounded wing tips. This is a well-proven wing form giving a solid structure and good aerodynamic properties across the whole span. This type of kite is for intermediate- to expert-level flyers because they develop phenomenal pull and lift. Many of these kites are good water performers but, likewise, many were originally developed for land use and are popular choices for buggy drivers, landboarders, snow kiters, and so on.

Don't attempt to use one of these kites on the water unless the manufacturer specifically states that the kite is appropriate for that activity. Large numbers of kites have subsequently been designed with more activity-specific features and limits. A typical higher-performance kite would normally be available in more and bigger sizes, reflecting the extremes and range of conditions you need to understand when you start to play with these very serious "toys."

Sophisticated drawing-board tinkering and field testing by design teams have ensured that all sizes of a particular model handle similarly, making it simple to switch kite because of a wind change. High-performance power kites often have a thinner profile to reduce drag and make them faster, and the wing tips have a thinner aerofoil section, improving the kite's turn speed. High performance, just like in your car, often means more response. The kites are more sensitive to steering controls and less forgiving of pilot error. Water versions appeared with anti-return valves on the inlet vents to prevent water entering if the kite landed on the water, vents to empty water and sand out. In the end the ram air's limitation as far as water use is concerned has been re-launchability from the water. But on snow or dry land there's no question

that four-line ram air kites have what it takes to be not just competitive but market leaders.

You can use them equally well out of a buggy or off the water, flying them for fun or as part of your power kite education. Of course it's always a good idea to familiarize yourself totally with every new kite you fly. This is the only way to approach the added risks of buggies and boards, so inevitably you're going to end up flying the kite simply as a kite for a good period at some point. You'll find that you'll be able to skid and jump as before, much more in fact as now the chances are you'll be flying bigger wings to suit your changing traction habits and your ever-increasing command of the kites and their power. But a vast range of other traction possibilities awaits you once you're into four-line foils.

Many four-line power kites can be flown using a choice of either control bar or independent handles. Different activities may be better suited to different systems so make sure you discuss the options thoroughly with your dealer before purchasing, and make sure they actually give you the correct kite.

With some kites, such as the Blade, an extra bonus is that the control bar can be used with either the four-line set-up, or with a two-line conversion-kit set-up you can fit to the kite. Some board riders (kiteboarder Chris Calthrop included) prefer the simplicity of two-line flying, the combination of stability and speed of a ram air kite ideally suited to their style of boardriding. Many other designs don't incorporate that feature and are always a four-line kite no matter which control system you choose.

Using a control bar is enormously different from using independent handles. If you're used to flying your four-line power kite on independent handles and decide to switch to using a control bar, make sure you familiarize yourself fully with the differences in the handling of your kite before you try any serious traction action.

Set-up and Pack-up Procedures

When you buy a serious quad-line power kite, it should come in a proper, heavy-duty carry bag with space for your handles or bar as well as the kite. Inside the bag the minimum you should expect to find is the kite (neatly folded), a pair of four-line control handles or a control bar with color-coded flying lines, and some kind of an instruction manual.

▶ *Kite control is a feature of quad-line flying*

A good manufacturer will include a product guarantee, but there's no guarantee of that. If any of these items is missing contact your dealer or the manufacturer immediately.

As with any new kite, you are well advised to go home and take the kite out in the calm comfort of your living room and have a good look at it there before you take the often sizeable sail out to a windy flying field or beach. Nine square meters of kite sail fed with some strong gusty wind can all too easily turn into a flapping monster, specially if you are holding the instruction book in your teeth at the same time. You will also need to make sure you have appropriate-strength flying lines for your new kite – make sure you ask your dealer for the right ones. A good, well-produced kite will include its line pack, obviously, but will also give you the recommended line strengths needed for average use. "Average" in this instance usually means dry land-based activities with relatively low resistance, such as buggying, landboarding, or snow kiting. For more serious traction activities, such as kiteboarding on water, or for use in very strong winds, you may need to upgrade your flying lines, in which case contact your dealer.

Follow the manufacturer's instructions for setting up and packing up and you shouldn't have a problem. In the unlikely event that you do, take the kite back to your local dealer for advice or contact the manufacturer direct; their details should be somewhere on the kite or instruction manual. Any manufacturer who's hiding their contact details clearly has something more serious to hide! Try to remember how the kite was packed when leaving the factory when you first unfold it, and try always to re-pack it the same way. Your instruction manual should explain how to set up your flying lines and attach your control handles or control bar. You will need to be familiar with the lark's head knot to attach your flying lines correctly so if you skipped that bit of the earlier section covering basic power kites, it's time to go back to page 32. *See also* Chapter 8 of this book for other recommended storage and packing tips.

Increasing numbers of power kites come fitted with a safety leash, which you should use at all times, whether you fly them using handles or a control bar. The system is normally quite straightforward to use, with a simple cord coming from the handles or bar attaching to your wrist by a velcro strap. The leash is attached to the brake or rear lines. Using handles you will usually have one safety leash for each handle or wrist. Using a control bar there is often just one leash; it's up to you which wrist you attach it to. The safety leash can be actioned any time you feel that the situation you're in or getting into is too much for you to deal with – the classic case being that you are over-powered and going too fast for comfort. If all other attempts to control the kite fail you simply let go of the handles or bar. The leash pulls on the brake lines of your kite but the front lines are released, spilling all air virtually instantaneously from the kite, de-powering it almost completely, and bringing it harmlessly back down to land or water. It's easy then to recover the controls and re-launch your kite. A few practice tries will soon have it under manners and will prepare you for when you need to use it for real. The safety leash is there for your and for other site users' safety – make sure you always use it.

Having fastened your velcro straps to set the safety leash, make sure your open space is still free of other people and obstacles and check that the wind hasn't changed direction, it can be very shifty at times, specially inland. It's recommended that you make your first few flights in light to moderate wind until you get used to how the kite handles and pulls. If it's all looking good at this point, you're ready to fly.

Flying The Kites Using Independent Handles

Launching

Under normal circumstances you should be able to solo launch as follows:

- Pick up the handles, remembering to put your ground stake in one pocket as you'll need it later to immobilize the kite and lines again.
- Take one handle in each hand, holding them firmly by the foam-cushioned section at the top, curve away from you and the bottom of the handles further towards the kite than the top. The front flying line leaders should come out from between your index and second fingers, and your thumbs should be on top of the handle, joystick style. This is the "neutral" position for normal flight.
- Make a last minute check that your lines are connected correctly, left to left and right to right, top to top, and so on, and untwisted. The wind should be on your back, with you and the kite in center window. The kite should still be on its back and the trailing edge weighted down.
- Pull back gently and steadily with both handles keeping equal pressure on all four

▶ *The correct ready for take-off position*

lines. The front or leading edge of the kite will lift up and the kite begin to inflate with wind pressure. As it inflates the kite will stand up on its trailing edge ready to take off. You can hold it at this point by pushing forward slightly with both thumbs until you're absolutely ready for flying.

- Pull sharply on all four lines to inflate the kite fully and it will start to lift off. You may need to take a few steps back to get it moving depending on the wind conditions. The kite will fly straight up the wind window as long as you pull evenly on all four lines, through the power zone, to come to a rest with minimum power in the park position at the top center or zenith of

the window. Be ready to deal with the pull as the kite hits the power zone, leaning back with your shoulders and moving forwards a little on the ground.

Let's take a quick look at the other solo launch method and assisted launching. In strong winds it's inadvisable to launch in center window as the kite will hit the strongest power zone of the window immediately after launch and can be very dangerous for you and other people. If there are strong winds:

- Set the kite up close to the edge of the wind window in relation to where you stand at window center. Lay the kite on its back, but this time lengthways downwind so that the wind blows across the kite from tip to tip, leading edge vents facing towards the edge of the window.

- Weight down the upwind tip with sand or similar, leaving the downwind tip free.
- Pick up your handles and pull gently on the downwind end of the kite (the tip furthest away), which will lift the tip and leading edge enough to allow the kite to inflate.
- Keep pulling steadily with the downwind handle and the kite will launch and fly itself towards the edge of the wind window.
- Keep pulling slightly on the downwind handle and steer the kite carefully up the edge of the wind window to the zenith, where you can neutralize your steering and get ready for action.

If using an assisted launch, make sure your helper understands what to do:

- First of all the helper should stand towards the edge of the window, behind the kite, holding it up so that the leading edge is facing the wind, pointing towards the edge of the wind window.
- Once the kite is inflated and you're ready, call to your helper to release the kite, simply

▶ *Top: Solo launch*
▶ *Bottom: Assisted launch*

letting it go rather than trying to throw the kite up, which will actually prevent a smooth take off. As your helper releases the kite, fly it out of their hands pulling slightly on the upper tip to steer the kite up the edge of the wind window to the zenith.

Flying

You can hold the kite at the zenith for as long as you like but as soon as you're ready you should start some basic turns. To begin with, keep the kite high in the wind window and make gentle control movements. This will keep it out of the extreme pull of the power zone while you get used to handling it. The basic turn maneuver is similar to a two-line kite:

- When the kite is climbing up the middle of the wind window and is nearing the zenith, pull back on the right handle keeping tension on both lines. The kite turns to the right and starts making a wide, full loop in that direction.
- Keep pulling on the right handle until the kite has flown a complete circle and is climbing up the wind window again, pointing straight up.
- Bring your handles back to the neutral position and the kite flies straight up.

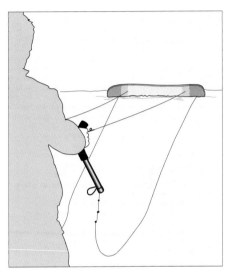

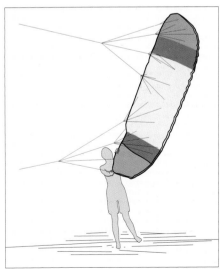

■ Now pull on the left handle to execute a left loop and untwist your flying lines.

You will find that as much as you pull with one handle you push with the other because of the angle of your body and this in fact makes a good, smooth turn. A pull with one hand "stalls" one side of the kite and the other speeds up around it. Pushing with the opposite hand makes a similar but smoother turn by keeping the whole kite moving. You can also start to make different and even better turns by using the extra control possibilities of the two extra lines, like this:

■ As you begin a loop, whichever handle is being pulled should be pivoted so that the rear line is pulled as well as the top. Push your thumb away from you and point the top of the handle more towards the kite. The kite will turn faster, even spin on its axis, before resuming full power.
■ As the kite comes round full circle, bring the handles back to the neutral position to resume normal flying.

As your flying becomes more confident you can experiment with more power. Flying alternate left and right loops in a kind of flat figure eight in the center of

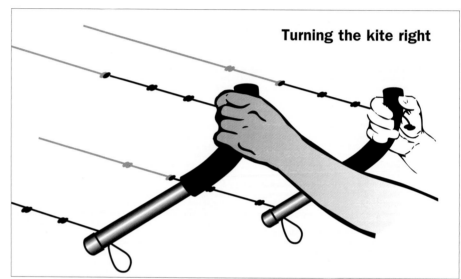

Turning the kite right

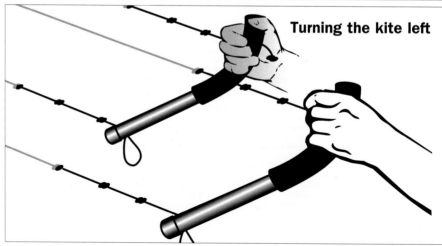

Turning the kite left

the wind window will give the best and most consistent pull as a fixed flyer (as opposed to one moving on a board, buggy, and so on) and stop the lines twisting too much.

Four-line control with handles gives you the ability to stop and reverse the kite, and even de-power it if needed. It requires a lot of wrist action and brings the rear lines fully into play. You stop the kite in mid-air by changing the aerodynamics:

- With the kite flying up the middle of the window, leading edge pointing straight up, rotate both handles by pointing your thumbs forward until the kite "brakes".
- Keep pulling on the rear lines and the kite slows to a stop and starts to reverse.
- To resume normal flying, rotate the handles back to the neutral position by bringing your thumbs towards you again and pull on the front lines.

With experience you'll be able to control the rear lines much better. Fine adjustments of your braking and playing the handles a little will enable you to position and hold the kite just where you want it almost anywhere in the window.

▶ Top: Practicing left and right loops
▶ Bottom: ... and ground-skimming low passes with a high aspect ratio 'Tsunami'

Landing

Landing is an extended version of stopping and reversing the kite. Technically it can be done anywhere in the wind window as long as the leading edge is pointing up. In practice you may find that it's easier to begin with trying it nearer to the edge of the wind window where there's less power in the sail. Be careful though – too close to the edge could make the kite unstable and require some juggling to keep it steady. Follow these instructions for landing:

- With the kite pointing straight up, as close to the ground as you can and your handles in the neutral position, apply almost full brakes by rotating both wrists so the top of the handles are pointing at the kite. You should be flying on virtually the brake lines only. The kite slows and stops very quickly, de-powering it.
- Keep the rear lines on full. The kite will descend backwards to the ground and settle on its trailing edge. Don't try to go too fast backwards or it may flip out, bottom towards you. You may well need to play the handles quite a lot, coming down the last few meters to keep the kite steady.

It will take a bit of practice to get right but, once you've landed, it's up to you

▲ The three stages of reverse landing

whether you want to re-launch or stop flying. Re-launch as you launched the first time. To immobilize the kite, peg the handles to the ground by the loops at the bottom, keeping tension on the rear lines as you do so. Then go and weight the kite down.

Re-launching And Recovering The Kite

Another advantage of four-line flying is that you can re-launch from almost any position. Generally you'll find that the kite is either on its trailing edge, in which case re-launch is obvious, or its leading edge (going forwards into the ground, making re-launch a little less obvious). But if you can reverse the kite in the sky, it logically follows that you can reverse it off the ground, too – what is known as reverse launching. Follow these instructions for reverse launching:

■ With the kite on the ground, fully inflated and standing on its leading edge, pull backwards (you may need to walk backwards a few steps) with the rear lines only. The kite should begin to rise backwards off the ground. You will often need to play the handles – thumbs pushed forward to disengage the top lines – to keep it going steadily.

■ Keep pulling back on the rear lines and when you judge the kite to have risen far enough to turn, push one of the rear lines forward by pivoting the handle and the kite will pivot too. It's easier to turn the kite up and away from window center rather than down towards it as the kite will tend to accelerate towards center window and into the ground.

■ When it's pointing straight up the window you can fly away or try another landing if that's what you were doing.

If that doesn't work there's another thing you can try. It involves turning the kite onto its trailing edge so the leading edge is pointing straight up, then you can re-launch in the usual way. This is normally easiest if you try to roll it over towards the window center. If the kite is directly downwind of you, walk a few paces to one side to create a new center window, which will automatically create a new position for the kite, closer to the edge of the window. Then:

■ Pull back on one handle only, the one connected to the side of the kite furthest from window center, the bottom of the handle more than the top. The tip of the kite will lift up and rise until the kite is standing vertically, leading edge pointing out of the wind window.

Reverse launching and landing

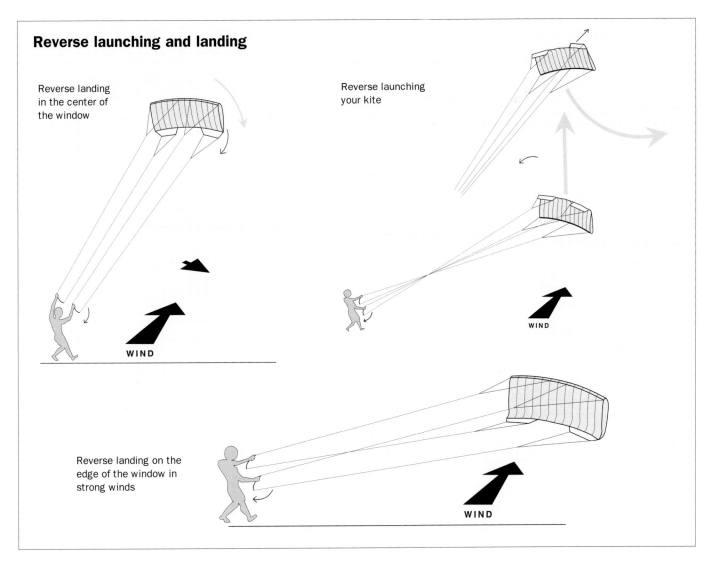

Reverse landing
in the center of
the window

Reverse launching
your kite

WIND

Reverse landing on the
edge of the window in
strong winds

WIND

- At this point you can start bringing the handle you pulled slowly back to the neutral position, still with more pressure on the bottom line. The kite should continue to roll down to a horizontal position, leading edge pointing upwards.
- As the kite reaches the correct position use your rear lines to keep it still on the ground while you get ready to launch in the normal way.

Troubleshooting

Under normal circumstances nothing should go wrong but if for any reason the kite doesn't perform, there are a few things you can check:

- Make sure that the bridles are not twisted.
- Make sure that the flying lines are correctly attached, heaviest lines on the front, left lines to left handle, and so on.
- Make sure that you've got the handles in the correct hands.
- Find out whether any of the lines have stretched. In fact, stretching can occur during your first few sessions, until the lines are fully flown in. Check your lines regularly to make sure they are still all the same length (see Chapter 8 for information about looking after your kit).

- If the kite is sluggish on take off and slow through the sky, the chances are that your brake lines are too short or main lines are too long.
- If the kite is unresponsive to steering and difficult to reverse, check that either the brake lines are too long or the main lines too short.
- In either of the above scenarios you can make an adjustment at the handles, shortening or lengthening them as appropriate, using the leader-line knots.
- If the tips or trailing edge are flapping there may be sand in the kite. Land the kite and empty the sand out through the vents at the front.
- If the kite still won't fly, contact your dealer or the manufacturer directly.

Expect to learn very quickly. Talk to other, more experienced flyers if you can. Their advice can save you an awful lot of learning-from-your-mistakes time. After a few sessions you'll be a fully competent power kite flyer and ready for some serious action.

Flying The Kites On A Control Bar

There's a growing number of power kiters who like the sophistication of top-range four-line kites with the simplicity of control bar flying. It's true that flying a kite on a control bar is in a sense simpler, but you sacrifice some control finesse with that. Yet a control bar makes a much better trapeze for aerial gymnastics. You could choose to fly with a two-line set-up as described. On the other hand there are those who prefer the four-line configuration on a control bar because it reduces kite speed but increases controllability. Flying four line on a control bar doesn't give you the full mobility of independent handles though, so you won't have the same control for reverse landing, for example.

There's also a significant number of power kiters who prefer to fly using a control bar because of the additional safety options and because it's better suited to the activity they want to do. For instance, snow kiting, landboarding and kiteboarding are generally easier using a control bar, whereas buggying is less of an option because with your body movement much more limited (sitting down) you couldn't get enough independent movement of your hands.

Most power kites that can be flown on a control bar have an appropriate model available, generally between 24 and 26 inches long. A general rule of thumb for beginners is to use a longer bar with a

◀ Peter Lynn Phantom

bigger kite and vice versa. Longer bars tend to make the kites more (possibly over) reactive. Make sure you get a control bar that is appropriate for your kite.

These days, all good control bars have a built-in safety system. This usually comprises a wrist leash attached to the rear (brake) lines sliding through an eyelet or slot in the center of the control bar. In the event of getting into unrecoverable difficulty, you can simply let go of the control bar. It will slide up as far as a stop on the rear lines, keeping these taut, and allowing front lines to extend and the kite sail to de-power itself, drifting harmlessly back to the ground and allowing you to recover it safely and with no bother.

Launching

Whichever kite you're flying, you're now ready to attach the lines or control bar as described in your instruction manual. Make sure the lines are untwisted and get your body in position ready to launch. You can solo launch in lighter winds but in a strong wind you must launch with a helper. In any event, you have less control over the kite and in decent wind will need to set up nearer the edge of the window. Follow these instructions for launching:

1. Lay the kite out on the ground (or have your helper hold the kite up to the wind) lengthways downwind with the leading edge facing the edge of the window. Weight the upwind tip down with sand leaving the downwind tip free.
2. Pull on the downwind (furthest away) tip with your control bar, pulling slowly and steadily. The free tip of the kite will begin to rise and the kite will start inflating as wind enters through the vents.
3. Keep pulling on the furthest tip (you may need to take a couple of steps back) and when the kite is fully inflated it will lift off and turn itself to face upwind or call to your helper to let go in the recommended manner.

   Steer the kite carefully up the edge of the window to the zenith by pulling gently on the upper tip of the kite with the control bar. Then bring the bar to a neutral position to park the kite.

Flying

As before, keep the kite high in the window while you get used to how it handles. Turning is done by pulling one side of the

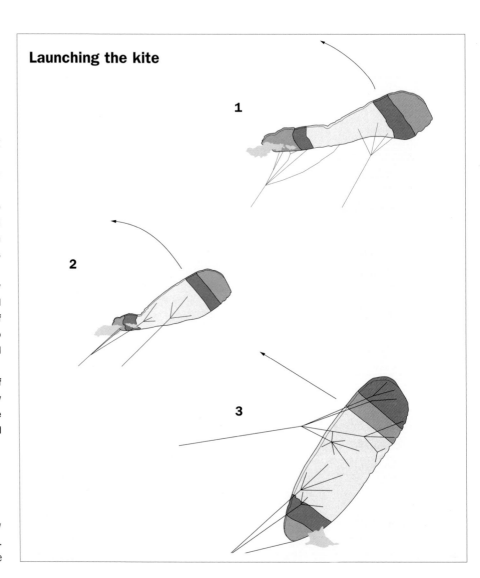

Launching the kite

bar towards you and pushing the other away, pivoting it around the center. Pull right to go right, pull left to go left. It will feel different from how the kite flies on handles so take some time to accustom yourself to its handling before you hit full power. But it's still the same kite and will perform in the same way, so far as how and where in the wind window it pulls. Practice some figure-eight maneuvers so you fly alternate left and right loops, making sure you can do it well to both sides.

Now that you're flying on a control bar you will not be able to slow the kite down, stop or reverse, so if at any stage you need to lose some power you will need to fly the kite out to the edge of the wind window, either at one side or at the zenith.

Landing

Without the ability to reverse land, this too will be done differently. You can self-land in light to moderate winds using the same technique as landing a basic two-line power kite if you wish:

- With the kite flying up the center of the wind window pull on one side of the control bar to execute a loop.
- When the kite has made half of its loop

and is pointing towards the other side of the wind window, bring the control bar to neutral and fly a (low) horizontal pass, taking the kite out to the side of the wind window it's facing.

- Keep flying the kite in that direction until it loses power, steering it towards the ground. It will fall to the ground when it is out of the window.
- Quickly go and retrieve your kite, weighting it down with sand or whatever comes to hand (but not sharp or pointed objects), otherwise it could easily blow away. If you are carrying a ground stake so much the better: put the stake firmly in the ground then hook the harness loop (if you've got a Blade bar) or the rear lines at the safety stop over the stake. This will apply the brake lines, immobilizing the kite, but you should still go and weight the kite down for maximum safety.

Or simply steer the kite from the zenith down the edge of the wind window (by pulling back slightly on one side of the control bar) until it comes to ground.

Do not attempt to self-land in a strong wind as you will almost certainly never be able to retrieve the kite before it blows away. You will need a helper to grab the kite and immobilize it for you:

- Fly the kite out to one side of the wind

window as described.
- Steer the kite down near to the ground.
- Your helper should approach the kite from downwind, behind it and well clear of the lines. Keep the kite as still as possible close to the ground until your helper is able to grab one tip and then pull the kite down.
- As soon as your helper has grabbed the kite you should release the tension on the flying lines by taking a couple of steps forwards. Once the helper has immobilized the kite by weighting it down with sand or whatever comes to hand you can stake down the control bar using the loop at the rear or rear-line stop if you wish.

"I was ecstatic when I realized I'd got my kite buggy idea to work. I was belting along this beach wondering if I was finally going to be able to quit my boring office job. I never dreamed the same basic design would still be going strong more than twenty years later."

PETER LYNN power kite and kite buggy pioneer designer

Kite Buggying

What is Kite Buggying?

The idea is very simple: fly a large single kite or stack of smaller ones, sufficient to generate enough power to pull yourself along. Sit in your vehicle and manipulate the kite in such a way as to pull you and it along. A modern power kite and kite buggy are sophisticated adrenaline sport tools, specifically designed for the job, generating speeds of up to 50mph, the result of more than 15 years of intensive commercial research and development. When you sit down in a kite buggy with the control handles in your hands you know you're in for a thrill and it's an immense buzz, travelling low down, open to the elements. Even your first 5mph run feels like 50. It's an up-to-date toy in all respects, but moving around by kite power is by no means a new idea. During the late 18th century, in the south west of England around Bristol, George Pocock was experimenting with kite traction using large kites attached to a carriage.

The First Buggies

Two hundred years later, long-standing kite traction addict and pioneer, New Zealander Peter Lynn, is widely credited with being the inventor of a successful modern kite vehicle. This time it's a single seat buggy or kart version, three-wheeled, with the driver sitting low to the ground over the rear axle, flying kites with his hands and steering the single front wheel with his feet.

This time the kite is a modern, two-lined, soft aerofoil kite, in Lynn's case called a Peel, on account of its pointed, eliptical shape making it resemble a slice of orange peel. The buggy frame is stainless steel and it uses high-quality bearings. Its simple basket-style webbing seat makes it very easy to be pulled out of the buggy, leading to many spectacular wipe-outs. The kites are not specifically designed for the job, they just happen to be what's available at the time. Kite power existed and people were hunting around for something to do with it. The whole package was far from perfect but, nevertheless, kite buggying was born and in essence has not changed format since, despite the countless buggies and traction kites there are on the market today.

The first Lynn buggies appeared in the mid to late 1980s, but manufacturing costs were so high they were very expensive, as were many of the kites to power them, putting them out of the reach of the average kite-flying Joe. Although the idea of buggying was sold as something you could do anywhere you could find a large, flat area, the reality was that clearly a buggy was most at home on big, hard, sandy beaches, or desert and salt flats, where the wind is smooth and you

▶ *An original Peter Lynn buggy*

can roll for literally miles. The buggy scene grew painfully slowly for a while, but grow it steadily did. Then in 1992 the first soft, four-line ram air kites appeared and other kite and buggy manufacturers were starting to get involved as the sales volumes slowly increased and shop prices therefore dropped. Large production-run buggy designs at cheaper prices were hitting the shops by 1994. Then Ray Merry and Cobra Kites launched their Skytiger four-line buggy kite in 1995, and suddenly buggying took off big time.

Within a couple of years a full national and international competition race circuit, club, and society network had grown up as all of a sudden kite buggying began to appeal to adrenaline sports people from beyond the kite scene. The surge of interest in the mid 1990s brought in new and different ideas, and equipment developed fast. Despite the rapid opening up of the power kite market, the likes of Peter Lynn and Flexifoil have been at the forefront of the whole traction scene, supporting events and organizations, and sponsoring drivers (and now kiteboarders). Products have developed at an astonishing rate and kite buggying is a vastly different beast nowadays compared

with its early years. For example, Peter Lynn – in common with most manufacturers active in the scene – now manufactures four different production buggies and has at least three kite models for different pilot skill levels and aspects of traction sports. New models appear every year and it's now a highly specialized, not to mention sizeable, business. Peter Lynn and Flexifoil have been joined by other manufacturers of high quality and high performance kite traction equipment, kites, and buggies. Manufacturers such as Advance, HQ, Invento, Libre, and Ozone have helped ensure that competition has been good for the market, pushing standards and performance to ever higher degrees.

How Buggies Have Developed

The latest buggies are designed for even more extreme use, especially speed racing and jumping or freestyling with the buggy. Race buggies tend to have wider rear axles and often the wheels angled slightly to improve stability at high speed; freestylers are shorter, tighter-turning and stronger to cope with heavy landings. You'll find there's a host of accessories available for you to customize your buggy for different terrains, meaning that a standard production buggy can be tuned for beginners and pros alike.

▲ *Top left: Libre standard buggy*

▶ *Top right: Libre 'Big-Foot' soft sand buggy*

Most modern buggies are crammed full with performance features and extras: an adjustable downtube on the front fork to cater to different sizes of rider, curved foot rests to help keep your feet in position, hi-grade wide stainless-steel tube frame for strength and stability, a wraparound seat and contoured frame for comfort and back support, stainless-steel bolts and specially engineered fittings, a splashguard for muddy fields and dirty beaches. They're absolutely right up to date, designed for maximum fun.

Buggying's natural beach habitat made it a logical next step to develop them so they could go on the water, too, as has now happened with kiteboarding, but you can argue that the water version would

never have happened without buggying sorting so many issues out beforehand. The surf version has somewhat eclipsed buggying of late, certainly in the media, but that can't hide the fact that more and more people are coming to buggying as part of the big wave of interest in kite traction tomfoolery. Britain and New Zealand are relatively small countries, but have lots of coastline and beaches. In the US we have a huge country but with proportionally much less beach and farther to travel to reach one if you live right in the center. That's why desert and flats buggying are so popular – in fact they provide the majority of the country's buggy playgrounds.

Buggying Safety

Let's say this now because before you go anywhere near a buggy you need to understand a few things:

- Good buggying means safe and responsible buggying, because the danger to yourself and other people is considerable.
- Do not attempt to kite buggy until you are proficient in using your kite.
- Never attach yourself permanently to the kite.
- Use extreme caution – never use your buggy in conditions that are too extreme for your skill level and equipment.
- Never kite buggy if you cannot safely handle the power of your kite. Use a smaller kite or wait for lighter wind.
- Avoid gusty winds, which can be very difficult for inexperienced flyers.
- Avoid all other kite contraindications (lightning, power cables, roads, airports, and so on).
- Always behave in a responsible manner and respect other site users.
- Always select a site with a big clear space all around you, free of people, obstructions and sharp objects.
- Always disable your kite and lines when not in use and avoid unsecured kites on the ground.
- Never buggy on busy beaches or anywhere you could injure someone, and always obtain permission to use the site if appropriate.

- Respect nature, the site, and other users at all times; always clear up your rubbish.
- Check all your equipment regularly (kites, buggy, flying lines, harness, and other safety gear) before use. Do not use worn or damaged equipment; repair or replace it immediately.
- Always use appropriate safety equipment.
- Be aware of your flying lines at all times. These can cause serious injury when under tension from a powered-up kite.
- Never allow inexperienced kite flyers to use your equipment.

You are responsible at all times for the safe operation of your kite, buggy, and other equipment. Take out third-party liability insurance that covers buggying. In short, use your common sense! There will be plenty of buzz to come without taking unnecessary risks.

How To Buggy

Starting

You'll want the right kind of kite for buggying and that almost certainly means four lines, so you can "lock" the kite in the power zone and regulate the power by changing the angle of attack. You should have a relatively thin profile to reduce lateral pull, a big wind window to

make getting back upwind easier, mobility around the window to guarantee continuous access to maximum power, good edge handling and performance, and smooth (as opposed to abrupt) acceleration to reduce the tendency to pull the driver out of the buggy. It's going to make the whole process a lot easier if you have a kite appropriate to your ability – there's no point buying a Ferrari if you don't know how to drive a car. Be honest about your skill level. If you're a beginner, try a beginner-level kite first.

It's possible to learn buggying on your own; after all, the people who invented it had to make it up as they went along, but a good idea might be to try one of the increasing numbers of buggy or wind-sport schools where you can learn the basics and try out different equipment in complete (and insured!) safety, before committing your cash.

At this point you will need to have your own buggy and there's no point suggesting a model. Let's just say there's plenty of choice and quality on the market. Follow the manufacturer's instructions for assembling whichever buggy you have. Make sure the wheels are tightly bolted on and the tires inflated to the correct pressure. There are three different widths of tires you can fit to your buggy. The most versatile are the standard width ones. Wide wheels spread the load over a broad area and prevent the buggy sinking in the sand. Even so, for very soft sand you might one day want to invest in a set of the giant extra-wide wheels that can be fitted onto buggies, though you may need to change your rear axle and front fork to do this. You might also want to change to an extra wide axle anyway; they improve stability and upwind performance, and are great for racing. The third, rarely used, option is narrow wheels, which are good for hard ground or even metalled road type surfaces such as old airfields. What's not so good on hard ground or roads is wiping out or being pulled out of your buggy.

As in all aspects of power kiting, you are best advised to start learning in a light to moderate wind, up to 15mph, as the kite will pull less and everything will be happening slower. You'll need to multifunction and there's definitely a bit of brain overload to begin with as you get used to controlling the kite and buggy simultaneously, so slowing everything down a bit can really help. Check the wind direction carefully, especially if you're using a coastal site. The best wind on a beach will be an onshore wind, coming onto the beach from the sea. Not only will it be smooth, as the aim will be to "sail" backwards and forwards across the wind,

it will allow you to run up and down the length of the beach and keep out of the water. An offshore wind will probably be lumpy and drive you out into the water more. A cross or side wind is the least-preferred option unless your'e on a beach with significant depth. Clearly you're going to need a vastly bigger space than ever before, especially while you're learning and can't fully control what you do. Here's how it should happen:

1 Your buggy should be pointing at 45 degrees to the direction of the wind, downwind to help you get going. Once the buggy is moving you will be trying to steer across the wind so as not to lose too much ground forwards. You can run downwind but you're going to have a long and uncomfortable walk back carrying all that equipment with the wind against you. Your first objective is to learn how to buggy across the wind.

How to get your buggy moving

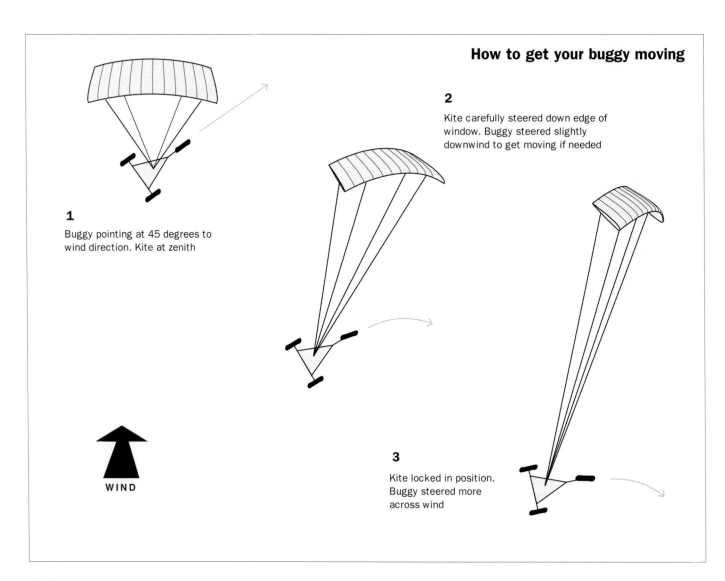

1

Buggy pointing at 45 degrees to wind direction. Kite at zenith

2

Kite carefully steered down edge of window. Buggy steered slightly downwind to get moving if needed

3

Kite locked in position. Buggy steered more across wind

WIND

- Launch your kite and take it to the minimum power position at the zenith while you approach the buggy from the downwind side. This is to avoid your suddenly being pulled forward by a big gust that might cause you to fall on the buggy.
- Keeping the kite at the zenith, straddle the buggy and sit down in it. At this point you still have some resistance from your feet.
- Put one foot (upwind) on its foot peg, the other still holding you from being pulled forward.

2 You are committed to going towards the side to which the buggy is pointing so carefully steer the kite down the edge of the window you want to go towards. Never take the kite back to the other side of the window as this will result in your being pulled backwards out of the buggy.

- As you feel the power coming into the kite, lift your other foot up onto its foot peg and steer slightly downwind to get the buggy moving.

3 Lock the kite in position at roughly 45 degrees to the ground and keep tension on the flying lines as the buggy gets going to avoid running over your own lines. Try to steer the buggy more across the wind. Remember to watch where you're going as well as the kite. You should be flying on the front lines mostly, just using the rear lines to keep the tension and hold the kite in position. If you're going too fast or feel there's too much power, take the kite further up the wind window, which will reduce power and slow you down.

- Keeping moving is easier in reasonable steady wind than in light wind. As the kite comes down the edge of the wind window it wants to power you in that direction. You lock your kite at 45 degrees to the ground and try to steer the buggy slightly up and across the wind. In a light wind you will need to work the kite more, flying a continuous figure-eight pattern on the edge of the window. This is easier said than done when you're also steering the buggy, watching for other site users, and so on.

The tuning of your four-line kite becomes quickly apparent, giving, if it's been set up correctly, the ability to hit the brakes very hard for an instant de-power, even to land the kite if it all gets too much. But, more significantly, it's the four-line control that allows you to lock the kite in position. And that's why four-line kites are so popular, helping you reduce the brain overload and concentrate more on buggying.

Another factor that comes into play once you start moving forwards across the wind is the phenomenon of "apparent wind." Imagine you are sitting in the buggy, pointing at right angles to the wind (wind blowing from one side). The kite is above your head and as you steer it down the window edge, so you bring it in front of the buggy and it starts to pull you along. As you speed up, the wind will appear to come more from in front of you, blowing into your face. The combination of the true wind and the wind from your forward motion is called the apparent wind. Buggying at right angles to the true wind, the apparent wind will increase the faster you go, causing the kite to pull harder, increasing your speed even more. Steering slightly upwind gives the optimum apparent wind but be careful not to steer yourself too far upwind and lose power as a result. To complicate things still further, not only will apparent wind blow harder, it will come more from in front, causing the kite to fly more downwind of you. The result of this could eventually be a big sideways skid or your being pulled out of the buggy sideways. Take pre-emptive action, moving the kite higher in the window to lose power and a little speed. And start your run aiming for a point just upwind of where you actually want to go to allow for this sideways pull. Kites that move around a lot (for example, two-line kites) will have a more variable apparent wind and less consistent power.

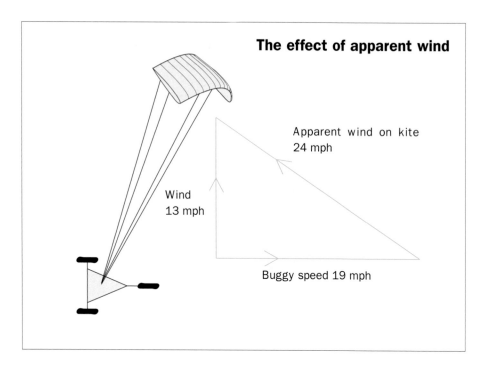

The effect of apparent wind

Apparent wind on kite
24 mph

Wind
13 mph

Buggy speed 19 mph

■ Stop the kite high up in the center window, pointing upwards (not across the window) and steer the buggy a little more upwind. The more you resist the kite the more you slow down. You will come to a stop with the kite flying just behind you above your head, in the minimum power position.

It's not a car, remember, so you don't just hit the brakes and wait for the ABS to kick in. It will be more of a gradual slowing down at first. It's all a question of timing and one part in particular of the timing is crucial. With the kite flying behind you there is a big possibility you will be pulled out of the buggy, or along in the buggy, backwards. Take the kite too quickly behind you, too far behind or with too much power and you're in trouble. The only thing then is to try and land the kite (easier said than done, travelling backwards at 15mph with your head banging on the ground) or let go of it altogether.

A quicker stop can be made with practice. It involves what is essentially the same maneuver but made at more speed and with more aggressive steering of the buggy. The main thing is to try steering the kite slightly more behind you at the top of the wind window and to do it fractionally (but only fractionally) earlier, at the same time turning the buggy more aggressively upwind into a skid. At speed

Stopping

Do not under any circumstances try and stop the buggy by putting your feet down on the ground while moving along. The chances of catapulting yourself from the buggy or breaking an ankle are very high. There's a perfectly simple way of slowing down and stopping that you should start practising as soon as you start learning how to move:

■ While driving along, across, down or upwind, start steering the kite up the edge of the wind window, pointing straight up. This is done by pulling equally on the two lines attached to the tip that is highest in the window, assuming you have the kite almost vertical on the edge of the window, so you pull back in fact with one handle. At the same time start steering the buggy a little upwind. The kite will begin to lose power and the buggy will slow down.

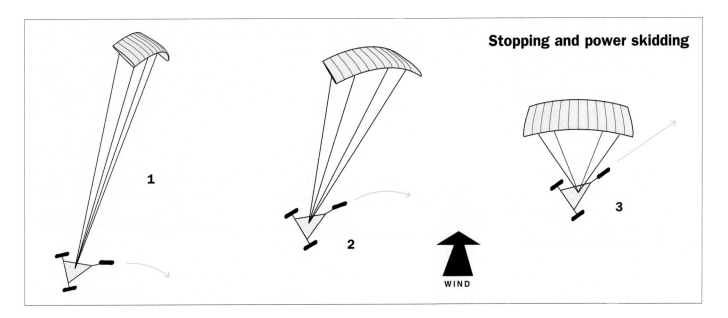

Stopping and power skidding

1

2

3

WIND

you slide the buggy to a stop facing upwind. Trying the fast stop means stopping with more power in the kite for you to lean against and hence there is more possibility of being pulled backwards out of the buggy. You'll need to keep an eye on your kite all the time once you've stopped or it may power up again.

Once you've learned the power stop, why not try a few power skids – the buggy equivalent of the hand-brake turn? You're probably going to end up doing a few inadvertently, anyway, taking into account the effect of apparent wind as described

earlier – that moment when the kite is flying so far downwind of you that you are pulled sideways in a big skid, fighting with an opposite lock on your steering. Power skidding is easier on sand and dirt, needless to say, but perfectly possible on grass, especially when it's wet or the ground soft:

■ Drive the buggy on a reach across the wind with the kite powered-up and locked in position at 45 degrees to the ground on the edge of the wind window.

■ Begin flying the kite up the window and slightly behind you as for a power stop. At

the same time slam the buggy into an aggressive upwind turn and immediately reverse lock your steering.

■ Keep the kite slightly less high behind than you would to come to a stop and then turn it back towards the edge of the window it was on, flying across the top of the wind window.

■ Move the kite into position on the edge of the window and as it begins to power up again let the buggy get going downwind a little then neutralize your steering to allow it to pick up speed before steering back onto a cross-wind reach.

Your ultimate sanction for stopping is to drop your control handles, releasing the kite and its pressure and allowing the buggy to roll gently to a stop. Or you turn the buggy upwind to stop sooner. This is normally not at all recommended as your kite and flying lines could seriously injure someone else on their way to the ground and will almost certainly be in an incredible mess when you eventually catch up with them again, wherever they've blown away to. And until the kite can be immobilized it represents a danger to other site users, including other buggy drivers. It could take out anyone in the immediate vicinity on its way to ground. Apart from all the safety issues, your quad line set spaghetti-ed around someone else's axles or flying lines is normally considered a gross breach of buggy etiquette.

As was mentioned earlier in the book, many power kites now come fitted with an emergency safety leash as standard, so you can now let go completely of your handles, safe in the knowledge that the kite will de-power and then return to ground with minimal risk to yourself and others. Recovering and re-launching the kite afterwards is relatively simple. Always attach your safety leash(es) before buggying and practice your emergency drill before you have to use it for real. Even the pro pilots can get into diffi-

culty and they would be the first to stress the importance of safe buggying.

You may occasionally be forced to stop if your kite becomes waterlogged, either from rain or some unintentional landings on the wet part of the beach. There's no option here: you must take it back somewhere dry, dry it out thoroughly and empty any sand out from inside before re-launching.

Jibing: Turning the Buggy Around

However you spell it, jibing means turning the buggy through 180 degrees to go back the way you came, which, no matter how good a time you're having buggying off into the sunset, you will have to do sometime. And, thinking about it, it's not at all obvious. The kite's in front of you, nicely powered up, what do you do with it next to get it back to the other side of the wind window without being pulled out of the buggy? And which way do you turn the buggy, anyway: up or downwind? My car's four miles back up the beach. Help!

You can turn up or downwind but upwind is an advanced technique so we'll concentrate on the downwind version. Like all maneuvers, it's one that needs good timing and adjustment all the way through. The first and most important thing you'll need to adjust is your forward speed. You can't really learn how to turn

going in at full speed so you'll need to lose some before you go in. The main thing to remember is always to turn downwind, towards the kite. You need to turn the buggy as quickly as possible. Actually turning the buggy is very easy as your feet are steering directly through the front wheel. There's no counter steering against the pull. Here are the instructions for jibing:

1/2 You are driving your buggy on a crosswind reach with the kite powered-up and locked at 45 degrees to the ground. Start steering the buggy slightly upwind and the kite up the edge of the wind window towards the zenith. The power eases off a little and the buggy starts to lose speed.

3 You're ready to make your turn. Steer the kite back up the wind window to the center, leading edge pointing straight upwards. At the same time steer the buggy hard into the turn. You need to use a full lock to bring the buggy round quickly.

4 As the buggy comes round 180 degrees and is pointing back the way you came, start steering the kite over to the other side of the wind window, the side you want to move towards, to power it up again and drive you through the turn.

5 Let the buggy get going again downwind slightly, then neutralize your buggy

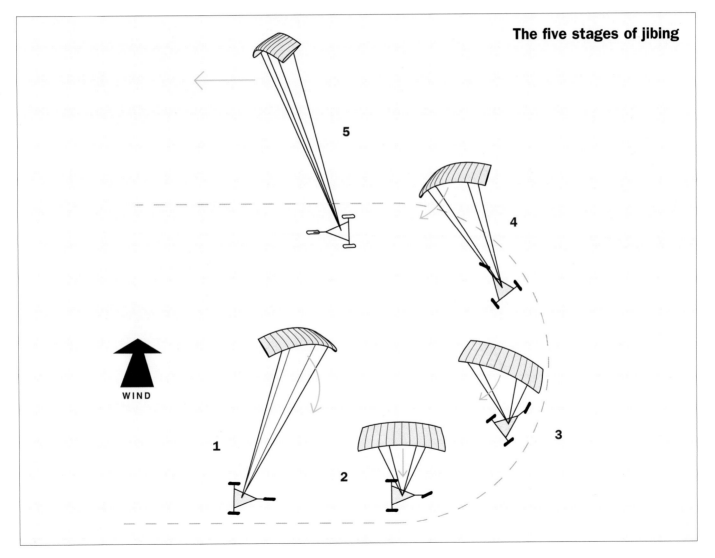

The five stages of jibing

1

2

3

4

5

WIND

steering and steer the kite to the correct position to lock it on the edge for your return reach. Be ready for the pull coming back on as the kite powers back up again.

There's a fine balance to strike to make a good turn. You must slow down beforehand but, above all, you want to go in with enough speed to get all the way through the turn in one hit. If the buggy stops moving then the moment when the kite powers up again is when you could be yanked face forwards out of and across your buggy.

As you make your downwind turn you come briefly face on to the kite. If you travel too far downwind or too fast you will de-power the kite, causing it to deflate and start to fall from the sky. Two things are likely to happen then. First, as the kite sinks, your flying lines fall on the ground, you run over them with the buggy and, hey presto, 293 twists of line around your axle. Second, with no kite to pull it, the buggy slows down, the wind blows on the kite bringing tension back onto the flying lines, the kite re-inflates and the power kicks back in... But now it's low down in the window, right in the power zone, and pulls you face forwards out of your buggy as it does so. If both of these happen then you're in big trouble as the kite will be almost impossible to control

with its lines snagged round the axle. You will have to forget about the handles and try to retrieve and control the kite before you can sort out the mess.

Most people's problems with turning arise from lack of forward speed going in, or from going too far downwind in the turn. With practice you'll be able to make your turns faster, keeping the kite moving all through the move and with more power, and clearly you're going to need to practice turning to both sides, for your own convenience and in case of needing to take emergency avoiding action.

An American kite flying legend called David Brittain, presently 100% hooked on kiteboarding and living in Europe at one of the top kiteboarding spots, a man who can fly a quad-line foil, ride a unicycle and juggle all at the same time (and has now started juggling on his kiteboard!), has developed a brilliant five-step learning system for would-be buggy drivers. It worked for me so I can recommend it, and it's incredibly simple. You only progress a step when you've fully learned the one before:

■ Step 1 – learn to fly your quad-line kite with accurate enough control to be able to position it at the zenith (12 o'clock) and fly it to each hour point in turn to both sides, returning each time to 12.

■ Step 2 – set out two cones on the ground about 50 meters apart, across the wind; walk a figure eight between and around the two cones, imagining or visualizing maneuvering the kite as you would in a buggy and making downwind turns round each cone.

■ Step 3 – do the same thing but now you really do fly the kite, wearing and hooking into your harness if you wish, using the kite's power to pull you around the course.

■ Step 4 – learn to make the same figure eight around the cones, now sitting in the buggy, but without the kite; you'll need someone to push you and this is your chance to learn how to steer the buggy without the added complication of the kite.

■ Step 5 – put the whole thing together, driving the buggy using the kite to pull you, using the smallest kite you have that will actually move you in the buggy; this will teach you how to work a kite for power.

A couple of steady afternoons spent learning all that and then making some longer runs will build your confidence and teach you how to control and use your kite's power. Soon you'll be ready for some power turns, which also come a lot easier if you feel confident about stopping and sliding your buggy. The difference here is that you're going to be sliding downwind, towards the kite. If you want to make a power turn:

- Drive the buggy fast on a cross wind reach. Steer the kite quickly up the edge of the window and to a position high in the window, leading edge pointing straight up.
- As you do so, slam the buggy into a full 180 degree turn, steering the kite over to the other side of the window to its locked position where it will quickly power up again.
- Reverse your buggy steering to counter the pull, putting it into a skid. Then quickly neutralize the buggy steering to accelerate away from the turn on an opposite reach, bringing the kite to its 45 degree angle to the ground.

The trick is to be quick with the kite so that the moment when you are face on to the kite and it is powered-up passes quickly. The kite will still, briefly, be behind you, this time with more power. You will be powering into the corner and it will be more difficult to turn the buggy so you will need good leg strength and quick feet to whip the buggy round fast. And with more power you will need to lean against the kite, making a lot of work for your lower back and upper body. The advantage of a power turn is that, if you get it right, obviously it's much faster and you lose less ground downwind.

Getting Upwind

Once you've established enough control over what you're doing in the buggy to be able to reach backwards and forwards across the wind, you will want to learn how to turn that into steady upwind tacking, either for racing or simply to avoid the dreaded long walk back. However well you learn to get upwind it is always going to be slow progress and you must be patient and prepared to work the kite and buggy to get where you want to go. Be aware also that some kite designs are better able to get you upwind than others.

Getting back upwind is the hardest thing to learn as a buggy driver so if you find it difficult at first, stick with it, because patience will definitely bring its rewards. Initially, as you learn to drive you will find that your reaches take you gradually downwind. To get back upwind you will need to steer more aggressively with your feet, trying to keep the buggy pointing slightly upwind on each tack, at the same time being less aggressive with the kite. You need to keep the kite less powered up by keeping it higher than normal on the edge of the wind window. If the kite is too low in the sky or too powered-up you will find it hard to gain ground. And there's that apparent wind

▶ *4 wheel Big-Foot perfect for soft sand*

factor to consider also. Again there's a fine balance to achieve because if you're traveling too slowly and haven't got enough power you'll also find it difficult. This is particularly so during the turn at the end of each tack. The turns are made downwind as normal and if you lose speed or stop you're going to have to give up some of your hard-won ground upwind, going slightly downwind to get the buggy moving again. You need to make the turns as tight as possible, if you can, steering a little more upwind just before the turn and turning through more than 180 degrees to get on another upwind tack. If it sounds difficult that's because it is. But once you've become skilled at this you've got a full hand of buggy maneuvers, and a whole adventure playground of kite-powered possibilities will open up for you.

Essential Buggying Equipment

There's an awful lot more to good buggying than simply having a kite and a buggy. There are all sorts of other bits and pieces you might want to have that will make your buggying easier and more enjoyable. But it's not simply a question of fun: first and foremost there's the safety aspect, protecting yourself and others from the worst-case scenario, because you're play-ing with big power and anything can happen. When you see a race driver fully kitted-out nowadays, ready to race in all weathers, they may have as many as 50 different extra accessories on top of the essential kite and buggy.

These are the essential accessories:

■ a crash helmet to protect you from hitting other objects or being hit by the buggy
■ strong shoes – your feet take a lot of wear and tear
■ knee, elbow, and wrist guards, protecting vulnerable joints from knocks and hard landings
■ suitable eyewear, and sunglasses to protect from ultraviolet and glare, but more likely goggles to keep sand and spray out of your eyes
■ gloves
■ ground stake for immobilizing your kite
■ a splash guard
■ a safety leash.

These are optional:

■ waterproof clothing, some kind of a spray suit
■ thermal inner clothing
■ a face guard to protect from spray (fits onto the helmet) and a scarf to protect from spray (these can help prevent some nasty skin infections you pick up from some dirty coastal sites)
■ ankle straps with a ground stake sheath
■ a wind meter
■ a harness and harness loop, which are invaluable if you want to buggy for long periods or in really big winds; you should not consider trying a harness until you have fully learned the basic elements of kite buggying
■ large ground stake (dog stake or other) for keeping several different-sized kites immo-bilized but ready to fly at one time on days of changeable winds
■ line equalizer for quick testing if your flying lines have stretched and by how much
■ a chest protector
■ shin guards
■ a beach tent or cabana to store spare equipment in and to get out of the wind for a rest when you can't always take your vehicle onto the beach
■ a back rest, because buggying can be very hard work for your lower back
■ foot peg straps, which will help stop your feet bouncing off the pegs as you go over bumps or round turns
■ a speedometer so you know how fast you're going
■ a compass so you know in which direction you're going
■ a rear kit bag to carry spare kite and lines
■ extra-wide soft sand tires

- extra-wide axle to reduce sideways skid
- a buggy belt to strap yourself in for some jumps on the sand dunes or simply to hold you in under extreme power (which can be extremely dangerous)
- a tandem kit for attaching another buggy to the rear of your buggy (there is theoretically no limit to how many buggies could be attached in tandem)
- Teflon-based lubricant (bike chain spray) for maintenance of the bearings.

And that's without looking at all the things like spare control handles or bars and flying lines, spare buggy parts, toolkit, sailcloth repair tape and kits, flying line sleeving, and splicing kit... It goes without saying that kite buggying is not really a sport you can participate in using public transport – you'll be needing a car or small van at the very least.

▶ Top: Crash helmet and sun glasses
▶ Middles: Knee guards
▶ Bottom: Elbow guards
▶ Far right: Buggy with spray guard

❚❚ Snowkiting is a new radical sport. It mixes skiing, snowboarding and kitesurfing. The result is your own power to go where you like. You can access untracked powder, pull off massive airs and smooth landings, or you can just blast about freestyling. ❞

ROB WHITTALL Ozone Designer, professional paraglider pilot

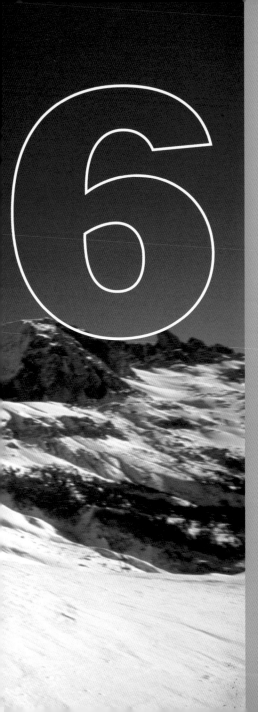

6 Other Land-based Activities

Once the basic principle of kite traction for wheeled transport became established, curiosity naturally drove people to experiment with various other options. Some things were obviously off-limits, such as biking, the ability to steer with your hands being somewhat crucial and in any event the center of balance being too high. Skateboarding was never really a contender, just too fast and unstable – there's not enough board to lean against and again the center of gravity is high. But there's a dry landboard option you can try, one that's really booming in popularity now as a cheaper way of accessing the thrills of kiteboarding than going on the water.

Kite Landboarding

Like a big, off-road skateboard, landboards (also known as mountainboards or all-terrain boards) are great fun on any hard beach or big inland open space with reasonably smooth terrain, playing fields being the obvious option. A beach, with its advantages of space and smooth wind, is what you really want to help you learn quickly. Confined spaces, bumpy surfaces and lumpy winds can make life very tricky, taking into account the relatively small board surface to grip and high center of gravity. As usual you'll need a very big space, away from other people and obstacles, with plenty of room downwind in case you are pulled forward.

The same safety equipment as for buggying is recommended, with even more emphasis on the elbow, wrist and knee guards. What you won't want to begin with is a harness because if you are pulled over forwards, the hook and its fitting could cause you injury, pushing back against and into your abdomen. Later on you might decide to use a harness and it will certainly help lower the center of pull, so reducing wasted effort, and resulting in faster, more efficient boarding.

What was very much a minority activity in the traction kite scene as recently as 2001 is now one of the fastest growing. It's easy to understand why. First, there are now decades of skateboard and rollerskate or blade culture in the US, and people are much more interested generally in all those board, skate or surf sports. Almost the same sentence can be used in relation to power kiting, bringing two powerful movements together in one sport. And there's a third factor. Kiteboarding (on water) has become an international phenomenon, but getting together the equipment that you must have to kiteboard safely doesn't come cheap. Kite landboarding offers a lot of the same sensations – speed, power, jumps, adrenaline – on a vastly lower budget. Not least, you need a much

smaller kite to get you moving fast on a landboard than you do on a kiteboard, because the friction from those four small wheels is much less than that of the flat hull or hard edge of a kiteboard working into the water. And there's no need for expensive water re-launch capability for your kite either. Not only that, the skills you learn in kite landboarding will be very useful if and when you decide to take it all out onto the water. The standard of the boards being manufactured today has developed almost a fast and as far as their water counterparts. Landboarding, mountainboarding, and all-terrain boarding have been around for a few years, anyway; it's not as though the whole thing started completely from scratch yesterday.

As before, you'll be better off learning in a light to moderate wind where things will happen more slowly. You can afford to be much less powered up than for a buggy, especially on hard flat sand, as the resistance from a mountainboard is very low. Use a smaller kite to begin with, as there will be less lateral pull and you should find it easier to stay up on the board. Tacking and getting upwind are the objective. Most boards are basically flat, curving up at front and rear tips, with a grip mat on the deck for the feet. They have cushioned, neoprene foot-strap bindings, which obviously help with leverage, just as they do in kiteboarding and wind-surfing. Arguably it's better to learn without the bindings, learning the basics before you start fixing yourself to the board.

Some early landboards were three-wheelers. Three-wheeled boards have their single wheel at the rear and cannot reverse, making them a better option for downhill (without a kite). The problem is you'd need to learn to jibe a three wheeler (in the same way as you do a windsurf board or a directional kiteboard) if you want to turn round as they can't go in reverse. Four-wheeled boards are able to go in both directions, like a twin tip board for kiteboarding (see Chapter 7). Just as twin tips have made learning to kiteboard a much easier prospect for legions of newcomers to that sport, so the four-wheel landboard has become the essential tool for kite landboarders, eliminating the compulsory jibe but also opening up a whole new range of trick possibilities. And just like twin tips in kiteboarding, they've established a virtual monopoly of the market because they make it simpler to learn: you get your fun fix faster.

The Landboard Range

With the prospect of actually being able to make some money out of producing them, a number of manufacturers have turned their attention to landboards. Competition has been good for the market: prices have stayed steady and design has improved fast. Some manufacturers have been in un-powered landboards for some time. Others, such as Flexifoil – which has been the first kite company to release a specific kite–landboard range – have come from kiting. However they got there, they've brought their specialist knowledge to the table and the result is a feast of great gear for you to indulge yourselves in.

Most manufacturers now have a complete range of four-wheeled landboards, each adapted to a specific performance requirement and skill level. The majority have tough wood or fiber-glass composite decks or some kind of carbon composite, footstraps, and some come with a coil ankle leash as standard. In fact the wheels, trucks, and bindings are pretty much as you'd find on a standard landboard. The leash means that when you wipe out, your board won't disappear down the beach and won't present a possible risk to other landboarders. There are several good brands on the market nowadays and it shouldn't take too long to find a local dealer.

In that range of boards you'll usually find something for beginners that also has the performance to interest more

adventurous and experienced riders. These are good for learning to jump and giving an all-round smooth and well-balanced ride – shorter, more maneuverable board with touch-sensitive steering – the ideal kind of board for the more advanced rider who's looking for that bit of extra buzz to be had once you get into tricks and jumping. Its smaller size and lower weight will mean less drag in the air, maximizing air time to make more radical tricks such as spins, grabs, and flicks easier. Some trickboards now have a grab handle mounted in the center of the deck for greater grab and board-off technicality and creativity, taking kite landboarding into the realms of pure freestyle. These type of boards generally come with heavy-duty skate-type trucks, approximately 8 inch tires, nylon wheels, and have grip pads and foot straps on the deck. You will also find longer, wider boards, designed mainly for long-distance cruising and for racing. Longer boards give a well-balanced and controllable ride at high speeds. A longer wheelbase, deeper truck and slightly larger tires make for smooth riding, minimal rolling resistance and greater comfort on uneven ground. Longer boards are ideal for long runs, carving, enduro, and safari-type trips. And, if you get a chance, check out a two-wheeled board called the Dirtsurfer,

a unique ride, giving the feeling of working and edge, as you would a kiteboard in water – not to everyone's taste and a vastly different experience from four-wheel boarding.

Your complete landboard package should includes the deck, trucks, footstraps, deck grip pads, and wheels, plus an instruction manual. Some boards now come with extras like a board, a safety leash, and a tool or repair kit. If any of the items you should have is missing from your pack, contact your local dealer or the manufacturer immediately.

You will almost certainly need to mount the footstraps, trucks, wheels and leash yourself, preferably somewhere appropriate in your garage or house, or you could ask them to put it all together in the shop (depending on how busy they are). The beach is not the best place, with all that sand blowing about, getting in your glue and screw fittings. Once you've got it fully assembled and you're wearing the appropriate protective gear, you're ready to start experiencing the big buzz of kite landboarding.

Starting

Your final check before getting on the board is to see if you are regular or goofy. This determines which way you prefer to

stand and, in particular, which foot you place forwards when you stand to ride a board. If you don't know, have a friend shove you in the back. Whichever foot you use to save yourself is your lead foot and the other the supporting foot. Goofy is right-foot forward, regular left-foot forward. Start off by going towards your good side to make it easier. Now set up your board, as for a buggy start, pointing downwind across the window, at 45 degrees to the wind direction, towards your good side:

- **Launch your kite and fly it up to the minimum power position at the zenith.**
- **You will need to approach the board from one side or the other: from upwind you can see where you're putting your feet better – important if you've got bindings to get into, but could trip over the board if pulled by a gust; from downwind you won't trip over but you won't see where you put your feet so well. Try from upwind first and see which you prefer.**
- **Bring the kite down the edge of the window you want to move towards, taking care not to bring the kite too low and risk being pulled off as a result. The board should then move towards the kite and keep moving towards it as long as you keep the kite there. There's a lot of body work to be done, balancing and**

levering against the kite and you'll need a good flexed position, knees and arms slightly bent.

- Start by steering slightly downwind to get some momentum before gradually easing yourself onto a cross-wind reach. Do this by transferring weight slightly onto your heels.
- You can slow down any time by taking the kite higher in the wind window but you'll need to shift your balance to allow for the reduced pull. And you may need to work the kite in an S pattern up and down the window in marginal situations just to keep going.

Remember that apparent wind factor we explained earlier. It will affect you here just as it does on a buggy – the stronger the wind and the faster you decide to go, the greater the apparent wind. You will need either to adjust the board's steering or to move the kite slightly to compensate. All being well it shouldn't take much time before you learn to hold a cross-wind reach fairly comfortably. Just like buggying, that will bring up another couple of issues – those of turning and turning around.

Stopping

The simplest way to stop your mountainboard is, as explained, to steer the kite up to the zenith and keep it there while you slow to a stop. There is a way of stopping more quickly, similar to the way you stop a buggy:

- You are reaching across the wind at reasonable speed. Start steering the kite up the edge of the window towards the top of center wind window.
- As you do so, start applying pressure on the board with your heels to turn the board

- upwind, keeping the kite high in the middle of the wind window, pointing straight upwards where it will brake your forward speed.
- Lean slightly against the pull of the kite to stop your board. Keep the kite up at the zenith with minimum power.

With practice you'll be able to make the stop much more aggressive, moving the kite slightly earlier and more quickly, like in your buggy. Be careful not to get the kite too far behind you or too low down or move too quickly , all of which could lead to you being pulled backwards off the board.

Practice this range of basic landboard maneuvers until you're really confident. Think about taking a course at one of the many power kite schools there are now – it could well help speed up your learning processes. You'll need at least two sizes of kite if you want to landboard a lot, something for light winds, something smaller for medium to strong winds. You'll be amazed at the speed and aggressive carving you'll be able to achieve, leaning hard and hand dragging like a kiteboarder. In time you'll be ready to start going for some jumps and more complex direction transitions. Whatever level you aim to landboard at, remember always to attach your kite and board safety leashes, if fitted. If not fitted, think about fitting them!

Turning and Jibing

You'll quickly notice, and you'll already know if you've come from a skateboard or mountainboard background, that when you lean forwards or backwards on the board, the effect is to turn it. If you're riding regular, leaning forwards will turn you to your right and leaning back will turn you left (vice versa for goofy riders). It's the land equivalent of front and backside carving on a kiteboard or snowboard. Leaning backwards against the pull of the kite feels more natural whereas shifting your weight forwards with the pull to ride more frontside feels less secure. Experiment at first when you are not too powered-up, with small "weaves" while running in one direction, gently slaloming the board between an imaginary set of cones. Keep the kite relatively high on your frontside carves to avoid having to lean too far forward. As your skill level and confidence grow you'll gradually be able to carve faster, harder and more aggressively, using more sustained kite power through the turns, compensating with your body strength and position.

As far as turning the board around 180 degrees goes, you've got two choices. The first involves turning the board like a directional kiteboard or windsurfer, what's known as jibing (see Chapter 5). This is the old-fashioned way of turning around (and is the only way on a three-wheeled board without stopping and getting off), which, in a neat twist, has become a cool trick, as it involves coming out of the turn riding frontside. Confused?

Let's talk you through it. You're on a good straight run across the wind:

- **Transfer weight to your toes and the board will begin to turn downwind, towards the kite. Go carefully, not too much weight too quickly. You are aiming to do a wide, carving, downwind turn. It might be worth carving slightly upwind just beforehand so as not to lose ground downwind.**
- **As you begin to turn the board, fly the kite up the edge of the window, turning it to point the other way and gradually bringing it across the high part of the window to begin pulling you in the opposite direction, keeping tension on the flying lines.**
- **Keep the weight on your toes as the board comes around 180 degrees.**
- **Bring the kite to the appropriate position and lock it on the edge of the wind window. The kite will power up again and you will accelerate forwards, back the way you came.**
- **Keep your weight over your toes, leaning slightly forward, flying the kite over your left shoulder (right shoulder for goofies).**

It's all a question of timing and the more you practice the better your timing will be and you'll be able to make the whole thing in one sweeping movement. Don't

go for it too powered up at first but aim to keep the board moving all through the turn, as in a buggy jibe. If you do stop it will be difficult to keep your balance and power up again riding frontside. The advantage of this type of turn is that you keep moving all through the turn. The disadvantage is that you're now flying over your lead shoulder with your back to the kite and your weight forwards. It needs good balance and feel for the kite and will require some practice to get right. You'll need to turn around again or make a neat transition (a small jump with a half rotation of the legs to switch the board quickly) to get back to riding front-on to the kite again. To make that frontside turn you'll need to make the same movements with the kite but reversed. The tricky bit might be working the board with your front foot to initiate the turn, and shifting your balance completely from front to backside as you drive through it.

But a four-wheeled board, as we mentioned, is more like a twin tip kiteboard for water – it's symmetrical, so you can take advantage of its reversibility when it comes to turning around. Jibing is a skill and takes some learning. You can speed up the delivery of your fun by getting going twin tip style while you take your time learning to jibe and ride frontside later. For the second way of turning the board around all you need do is slow down, stop, then power up again in the opposite direction:

- **As you ride along, bring the kite up the wind window where it will act as a brake, slowing you down. Shift your weight slightly to the center of the board.**
- **Fly the kite across the top of the wind window, turning it to point the other way. As the board stops, bring your weight over onto your good foot so you are now leading with your bad one.**
- **As you bring the kite down the other edge of the window it will power up again and you can lock it at the appropriate place for your return reach. It's all in the timing again and practice will make for neater and more aggressive changes of direction.**

Whichever way you're doing it, with practice you'll be able to make your turns faster and more aggressive, losing less power and speed. You can also do other tricks such as jumps and power slides, specially once you start using bindings.

Snow Kiting

No university degrees handed out for guessing what this is all about. It seems fairly obvious that most things you can do on a waterboard or skis you should be able to do on a snowboard. After all, as the experts have been keen to point out, snow is simply frozen water.

Snow kiting is a sport that, considering its potential, like landboarding, developed less quickly than buggying and then, later on, kiteboarding. The huge surge of interest in all forms of traction possibility during the last five years has given snow kiting its chance to emerge into the public gaze and awareness. In fact, given the slowness with which the medium has been exploited until recently, arguably the fastest progress is currently being made by the ice and snow kite freaks. There is now an established winter competition tour, which visits sites in Europe and America, and a series of other events in America; this all helps to give the scene its momentum in terms of research and development, skill levels, exposure, and encouraging new people into the sport. Competitions tend to take one of two possible formats: freestyle (similar to kiteboard freestyle) and racing. Freestyle is all about tricks, transitions, big airs, and fluid riding. Racing is quite simply

about the fastest rider from A to B. With the growth in market similar to that experienced by kiteboarding a couple of years ago, manufacturers have been encouraged to design specific snow kite equipment (boards, wings, and so on) knowing that the sales volumes they need to make such projects viable are starting to arrive.

The snow kite scene is buzzing nowadays but there's nothing all that new about it. Back in the 1970s, around the time Merry and Jones were developing their Flexifoil concept, two Swiss skiers, Andreas Khun and Dieter Strasila, were experimenting with old parachutes they'd bought secondhand from NASA (them again), to see if they could be used to get up slopes not served by the chair lifts to ski back down. They called it para skiing. Later they used parapentes to achieve the same thing but with the added possibility of parapenting down or, better still, flying in and out of a snow kite spot on a parapente, which they could also use as their kite. That's probably one reason why a number of parapente manufacturers have now got involved in manufacturing ram air snow kiting and other traction wings. Ram air kites have been the most popular choice for snow kiting until recently, largely because of their extra maneuverability and the autonomy factor (you technically don't need a helper for the launch

© Bertrand Boone/www.flyzone.com

and landing phases). But increasing numbers of inflatable tube or "bubble" kites (see Chapter 7) are being seen on the snow now with some inflatables designed specifically for snow kiting. They've brought with them principles such as de-power systems (again, see Chapter 7), which have now been incorporated into ram air kite design. Some kite makers, such as North, have now released a ram air kite for snow use. It's all getting very confusing.

It's taken almost 30 years for Khun and Strasila's idea to take off but nowadays there are increasingly large numbers of riders on the snow each winter using ever-more sophisticated equipment. And the skill levels have developed enormously with it. Riders are trying many of the water freestyle tricks and huge jumps. But remember, although snow is just frozen water, it is a good deal harder and less forgiving. There's a risk of serious injury, as with skiing and power kiting. Always ride safely and use appropriate safety leashes and other devices where these are fitted.

There's a lot of attraction in snow kiting as a great winter alternative to kiteboarding, if you aren't lucky enough to have the kind of lifestyle that allows you to go chasing the sun every winter. The northern states of the US and vast tracts of Canada are the earthly form of snow kiters paradise. Huge empty spaces (think Wyoming, Montana, Idaho...) and low population or tourist density. Yum, yum! And that's without talking about other, more recognized, winter-sports centers (in nearby Colorado for instance), with which America is well blessed but where, as in Europe, it may be more difficult to snow kite because of the increased risks of and to the larger numbers or skiers and boarders. Check before you book. If you've booked your ten days off work, you don't want to be disappointed as you try to launch your kite in a place where kiting is not authorized.

If you do get into snow kiting you will need to develop three sets of skills to be able to ride safely: kite skills, board and ski skills, and a sense for the mountains and snow. The risks are enormous, especially off-piste, which is where most snow kiters will be; kites are banned at many recognized ski stations because of the potential safety risk they present to other skiers and boarders. There is the risk of avalanches or of falling badly, but also the risk of the weather closing in to cut off your route or simply losing yourself in the wide open spaces. And that's in addition to the normal risks presented by the flying of large traction kites and the wearing of skis or snowboards. You will need to be well protected and well prepared.

That means crash helmets, harness, warm clothing, goggles, gloves, and so on – as well as a spare kite, food, drink, map, ice axe, and some kind of GPS or avalanche rescue device.

There are a lot of kites on the market nowadays that are recommended for snow kiting. Not all of them were specifically designed for snow, but manufacturers such as Advance, North, Ozone, and Wipika now have high-quality, dedicated, and very refined snow-specific kites in their ranges. Almost (I use the term cautiously because there are always exceptions) any quad-line ram air kite will give you the autonomy and power you want. Low- or medium-performance kites are more suited to beginner riders because of their medium speed and stable handling. Also, with a lower maximum size, you're not going to be dealing with the bigger power that you will with a large, high-performance kite that the experts and pro riders have the skills to be able to use. High-performance ram airs, with faster speed and harder, more consistent pull, are more for intermediate to advanced riders. Bubble kites don't always give you the same autonomy as a ram air, meaning you may well need a helper for launching and landing.

On snow, as on water, you can choose to ride with independent handles (if it's a ram

air) or with a control bar. The same arguments apply as before: using handles gives you greater mobility and maneuverability of the kite; using the control bar is simpler, with more possibility for hand-free maneuvers such as grabbed jumps. If you already have a kite and are thinking of moving into snow kiting it's a good idea to check with your local dealer or the manufacturer whether your kite is suitable, or whether you should consider something more adapted to snow kiting with board or skis.

The ideal spot for learning snow kiting is a wide, open, flat expanse where the wind may be smoothest. Frozen lakes usually offer the best opportunities as these can extend for vast distances. If you're snow kiting in the mountains at altitude, be aware that the air is thinner and you may need more wind to get the power you want, but watch out for wind surges! Generally speaking, the friction on snow and ice is much less than on water and the power required to get moving needn't be too great. You'll also need to decide whether you want to ride a snowboard or use skis. The snowboard's similarity to a twin tip kiteboard makes it a good choice for winter kiteboarders, whereas people already into skis may well wish to stick with them. Learn without using the harness, flying smaller kites to begin with until you have completely learned the

basics, before you try attaching yourself to a bigger wing with much more power. Again, the best thing would be to go to a school and do a course – as usual it will accelerate your learning process. At present the best place to look for school contacts is in the kiteboard and power kite magazines or on the internet.

Starting

If you've already had a go at buggying, landboarding or kiteboarding then the basic principles won't be at all strange, other than the new medium. The method of generating power or traction with the kite is the same and there's a simple test beginners can do to determine which is the correct kite size. Launch your kite, put it at the zenith and if you can't walk backwards holding the kite there your kite is too big. Change down a size. Avoid going out over-powered. Inland wind, especially in the mountains, can be very gusty and changeable. If you're ripped out by a gust it could well mean the end of your session, day or even holiday. And don't overestimate your ability – try to be honest and you'll learn quicker. Finally, whether you're using a control bar or handles, a board or skis, always, always attach your safety leash(es). These are the basic instructions for getting started:

- Establish a safe area downwind of at least two line lengths. Unroll your kite and either weight it down with snow along the trailing edge (in moderate winds) or the upwind tip (stronger winds). In stronger winds you should set up near the edge of the wind window.
- If you're flying with handles, re-wind about four or five turns of the brake lines onto the handles; if you're on a control bar, pull the rear lines in as far as the stop, both of which will prevent the kite self-launching.
- When you're properly ready to launch, let out the brake lines and slowly move backwards until the front of the kite starts to lift up and the kite inflates with air (or the downwind tip if using the other method). Pause at this point and allow the kite to inflate as much as possible before take-off.
- You can launch the kite exactly the same way as described earlier in the book, allowing for yourself to be pulled some way forwards as the kite passes through the power zone of the window on its way up to the zenith. Learning to launch from and use the edge of the window can seem pointless but will in fact serve you well when it comes to dealing with stronger conditions and riding out wind surges. If you are using a harness, now is the time to hook in, before you get your skis or board on. Don't take your eyes off the kite for more than a second at a time.
- Be methodical about setting up and you'll

avoid endless to-ing and fro-ing untwisting lines, and so on. Try some test launches and landings before you get onto your board or skis to make sure everything's OK. To begin with you're going to get going downwind, just as in your buggy or on your landboard, before you start trying to work the edges of your skis or board and the kite's position to hold a line across the wind, which is the ultimate aim of the learning phase.

■ With your kite at the zenith and your skis or board on, bring the kite slowly down in front of you in the wind window – not too far, just enough to power it up and get you moving forwards. Be careful not to let the lines go slack as the kite will fold up and fall down the window, then pick up again viciously as the wind kicks back in. Try to dig the edges of your skis or board in to keep the line tension.

■ If you want to try and accelerate, fly a small S pattern with the kite. Once you've got some speed up, the apparent wind factor will begin to apply and you should be able to lock the kite in position towards the edge of the window with constant power.

■ While building the power in the kite, you should also be trying to work the edges of your skis or board further and further

▶ *Low aspect ratio ram air 'Wasp kite', ideal for your first runs*

around until you hit your "reach" line, across the wind.

It all comes down to good synchronization of these basic elements: holding a good line with your skis or board, acceleration, and speed. At all costs avoid taking the kite behind you, as this will almost certainly lead to an uncomfortable wipe-out. Without a doubt your first few runs will take you downwind, but, with practice, you will be able to get back upwind, just as you can in the other land activities.

Stopping

Across or downwind, there's also no doubt that at some stage you're going to need to slow down and stop without hurting yourself, preferably learning how to turn 180 degrees so you can make your return run back to your start point. Unless you skipped the earlier sections, you'll already have guessed roughly what's involved in all these maneuvers, as we're basically translating the same wind behaviour, kite principles, and rider skills from one activity to another. To slow down and stop:

- Dig your edge(s) in with heel pressure to turn slightly upwind.
- At the same time pull slightly on the upper tip of the kite to maneuver it back up the wind window towards the zenith. Again, be careful not to take the kite too far behind you or with any power.
- As the kite de-powers at the zenith you will gradually come to a stop.

Jibing

The 180 degree turn or jibe, as the buggy and kiteboarders have it, is a combination of all the elements you would expect if you've already done any skiing or boarding and had some power kite experience or read the earlier sections of this book. If you're a snowboarder there's no problem – you're riding a twin tip that can go backwards and forwards like a four-wheeled landboard. That way you can stay in the more natural position, riding backside, leaning back digging the upwind edge in. It's exactly the same maneuver with the kite as with the landboard, up the window to the zenith (careful not to let it get behind you), slow down to a stop and power up going back the other way, leading with your other foot. The same frontside option applies as it does to the landboard, though, meaning you could choose to turn more like a skier, actually shifting to the other edge and turning around to lead with the same foot on the frontside edge but flying blind over your leading shoulder. For a snowboarder a slalom is a series of back and frontside edge turns.

A turn through 180 degrees on snow should, as in your kite buggy, always be made downwind. The turn is initiated with the board or skis and you will need to try to drive through the turn smoothly and as fast as manageable to avoid de-winding the kite. Likewise, try not to turn too wide for the same reason, going in with reasonable but not excessive power, allowing you and the kite to get around comfortably:

- Initiate the move with your board or skis by gradually bringing them flat and adopting a more upright body position, with your weight moving over towards the downwind edge of your board or skis. Bring the kite up the wind window towards the zenith
- With the kite at the zenith there will be a moment when you are flat on the skis or board pointing downwind. Keep driving through the turn to avoid de-winding the kite. Bring your weight over the opposite edge of your skis to the one you were on or the frontside edge of your board.
- Power the kite up again by bringing it over to the edge of the window you wish to move towards and slightly down the window, working the edge(s) of your skis or board with heel or toe pressure to complete the turn.
- As you come out of the turn on skis you will

be leading with your other, upwind, foot flying front on to the kite and leaning back against the pull. On a snowboard you will now be riding on your toes, still leading with your good foot, but now leaning forwards and flying the kite over your lead shoulder.

With practice you'll soon be able to ski back and forward across the wind, and get upwind, until you've fully learned these basic elements. At that point you'll be ready to try some jumps, using the snow contours and wind currents to boost your airs, spotting your landings, and carving up the snow. Although we haven't gone as far as jumps here you'll find a section on jumping in Chapter 7, which gives you the same kite maneuvers. The rest is up to you. It's strongly recommended that you take a course in snow kiting at an accredited school, especially if you are thinking about taking it to a more serious level. Please make sure that you're fully protected before you try jumping on snow, as accidents can happen all too easily and you'll obviously have a few crashes during the learning phase. Enjoy your snow kiting but, most of all, enjoy it safely.

> **" The Wheels of Doom ride about 5mph faster than a buggy, you can use a bigger kite and lean harder against its pull to generate more power. I've ridden thousands of miles now and hit speeds of over 55mph! "**

**BOB CHILDS kiteskater,
inventor of the Wheels of Doom**

Kiteskating And Powered Blading

For the time being this one can still be filed under "interesting but strictly minority". But then that's what they said about kite-boarding and landboarding and look at them now. Kiteskating and powered blading means low resistance, high speed, and hard crashes. Not one for the faint hearted, full safety equipment recommended. Mostly done on a kind of mountain or landboard version of rollerskates or blades, using mountain or landboard wheels and a full-blade style boot. This is another kite traction area where one man

► *Kite low down for maximum power: Bob Childs on his Wheels of Doom*

has almost single-handedly championed the cause, an American traction freak currently living in Europe, Bob Childs.

Bob Childs is the Cory Roeseler of his sport. He's been kiteskating (his words) since the mid 1980s and, combining the best of Roeseler with the best of Peter Lynn, was the first to devise a workable kiteskate set-up. As with Lynn's buggy, Childs' innovation with skates has been much imitated and developed since but the basic format has never been bettered.

His Wheels Of Doom have been demo-ing at kite and extreme sports events in Europe and America for years and represent for him a serious commercial product. Check out the doomwheels website (www.doomwheels.com) for a more in-depth picture of the kiteskating scene and Bob Childs' leading role in it, plus a superb photo gallery to inspire your learning phase.

One or two other companies now manufacture something vaguely like kiteskates and you should try skate and

kite retailers as a first suggestion. If you find them difficult to track down, you're looking at a DIY project, in which case go back to the doomwheels site where Childs gives you details of how to do exactly that. You can try conventional rollers on tarmac if you like but it's hellishly fast and hurts a lot when you crash.

Blades and skates are a bit more like water skis and wakeboards, in so far as you strap yourself in first and then launch the kite to power yourself up. That in itself presents dangers because if you get into difficulty you cannot detach yourself from them, you will have to deal with the kite somehow. Saying that, clearly there is the potential to go very fast with such low resistance, and there's notionally more freedom of movement for jumps and tricks than with landboards. Time will tell.

Start with a small kite, sufficient to get you moving; until you have learned the basics with a small kite don't attempt it with a bigger one. Even so, being strapped in you don't want to launch the kite in center window with full power so you need to set things up carefully. Work out your regular or goofy stance and go in that direction to begin with as you will be leading with one foot. Pick a moderate wind day and, as before, objective one is to learn to ride backwards and forwards across the wind:

▲ Leaning into it on blades

- Set up the kite close to the edge of the wind window, on the side to which you want to go.
- Put your blades or skates on along with your other safety equipment and get ready to launch the kite, pointing yourself slightly downwind to help get some momentum. Your feet should be parallel, with your good foot slightly advanced. Another option would be to launch the kite sitting down and then use its pull to lift you once you've got the kite to the next stage.
- Launch and fly the kite straight up the edge to the zenith, balancing your body to lever against any pull. If you move forward a little don't worry, taking the kite to the

zenith will slow or stop you again.
- Now, bring the kite slowly down the edge of the wind window on the side you want to move towards. It will begin to power up and you will begin to move forwards. You will need to make lots of body adjustment to lever against the pull. Keep your knees bent, leaning back to lever against the kite. You may need to work the kite to keep just the right amount of power on, or off!

Stopping requires a similar technique as for the other land-based activities and needs practice to understand, then a lot more practice to be able to stop at exactly the moment or place you want...or need to! This is how you do it:

- Take the kite up the edge of the wind window towards the zenith, pointing straight up. The kite will be flying slightly behind you and will act as a brake. Don't let it get too far behind you or you risk a heavy fall backwards – take the kite higher in the window to lose power.
- Turn your skates to point further upwind, so you're flying over your shoulder. You will quickly come to a stop.
- Keep the kite at the zenith or land it right on the edge of the wind window.

An alternative to this would be to apply full reverse with your rear lines. This should de-power the kite immediately and you can turn the skates upwind while you reverse land the kite. It's a flashy but risky option as the kite may power up again before you can properly immobilize it.

Turning is done the same way as usual, downwind, similar to the way you turn a landboard or, better still, a kiteskier. With practice you'll be able to carve tighter, more aggressive turns, the small size and light weight of the skates making it easier to get over onto the other edge. You won't have the restriction that a board rider has of inhibited foot movement. Independent foot movement gives you the freedom to make rapid transitions with your feet while in motion, so that you're leading with your good or bad foot. This means you can choose to stay face on to the kite, using the twin tip idea but requiring you to lead with the bad foot, or stay leading with your good foot, coming out of the turn riding a cool frontside, leaning forward and flying over your lead shoulder.

We've only touched very lightly on the potential in kiteskating here, largely because that's exactly what power kiting itself has done up to now: just scratched the surface. It's an under-exploited format as things stand, but as has already been seen in power kiting, they don't always stay that way. If all the pioneers had lost their "try, try, and try again" spirit, power kites would never even have got off the ground in the first place. Kiteskating's day will come; people just need to see its possibilities.

Getting Big Airs With Tricks And Gymnastics

If you enjoy getting your airs in a big way you'll be looking for two things: distance and hang time. The biggest officially recorded jumps have been well over 100 feet and have been made with the help of full support and back-up teams, not to mention medical assistance being on hand if necessary. Stories of even bigger training and accidental jumps abound, with varying degrees of amazing escapes, broken bones, and sometimes more serious consequences. You can use big stacks of Flexis or big single traction foils, both will do the job. As we mentioned in the basic jumping section, four-line kites may not be a good bet as they are very responsive – fine on the ground but once you're up in the air the slightest pull on a handle or line could send the kite back into the power zone or collapse it completely. You may also wish to use a control bar, certainly if you're a kiteboarder trying to work out a move, as this will help you simulate the conditions you'll be in on your board.

The basic idea of the tricks is to start actually using your hang time, in the same way that kiteboarders are doing, to hit some rotations or whatever. Like everything else, try in moderate winds with some smaller airs to begin with. You will be landing on hard ground at speed. Build up the power and size of your jumps gradually as you gain skill and confidence. Single and multiple rotations and somersaults are the general order. Rotations in the air will lead to rotations in your flying lines, so you'll have to untwist them again afterwards, or pre-twist before lift off. The safest way to untwist them is to put the kite at the zenith and quickly spin yourself the appropriate way on the ground. Be careful: a kite big enough to get you airborne for several seconds could also lift you away in a gust or surge, even when parked.

Be aware that any sizeable jump is going to result in a very heavy landing, so you will need good spatial awareness to be able to spot your landings feet first rather than head first. And you must be fully protected with helmet, gloves, strong footwear, and elbow, knee, and wrist guards. It's very tiring and you won't be able to keep going too long. Especially as all your jumps will be taking you downwind, leaving you a stamina-sapping walk back upwind to your start point trying to keep your kite(s) at the zenith with no power. Acknowledging the somewhat unhinged nature of the activity, try even so to take care with getting your airs, just like all your other power kiting disciplines, and minimize the risk to you and others. That way you'll enjoy your power kiting to the maximum.

105

"If there's one thing in life you've got to try once, this is it. Kiteboarding is the ultimate sport for me!"

JASON FURNESS Flexifoil team kiteboarder

Kites for Sea and Surf

Leading Edge Inflatable Kites And Ram Airs

Throughout the short history of the sport, there's been much learned discussion and disagreement about when and where exactly kiteboarding was invented. What's not disputed is that people have been experimenting with kite power on water for years and that the current explosion of interest in this new most radical of extreme sports is the result of a long and winding journey to arrive where we are now. The potential was obviously there, if only the formula could be perfected. All over the world, people have tried all sorts of systems for getting onto the water with kites, including adapted buggies, floats fitted in place of the wheels. Of all these, Cory Roeseler's Kiteski rig, a single ski with a large, framed kite and a motorized winding, recovery or re-launch system flown on a control bar, which was up and running in 1993, was the most workable and the closest to what we recognize today as kiteboarding, but it was not commercially successful. The rig was ahead of its time in many ways and Roeseler, like other water pioneers, is still very much involved with the water kite scene.

The general consensus nowadays seems to be that the first successful kiteboarding as we understand it today took place in the south of France, on the coast near Montpellier, some time around 1996–97. From there it was exported, mainly by one man, Manu Bertin, to Hawaii, or more correctly Maui, to where the likes of legendary futuristic surfer Laird Hamilton and his group were also trying to make kiteboarding happen.

This small group of power kiters and surf freaks used adapted surf boards and the kind of big wings that were about at the time. Those mostly, with one notable exception, consisted of big ram air wings such as the two-line Peels, four-line Skytigers, and others that quickly followed. From France and Hawaii, kiteboarding has now been successfully exported to dozens of countries around the world.

Clearly there was one big issue that had not really cropped up in kiting before to any great extent, other than in an experimental or demonstration sense: water re-launching. A big ram air kite is made with big vents along the front, which take in water just as effectively as air. The ripstop fabric is covered with a waterproof coating but after more than a few minutes lying flat on the water the whole sail becomes waterlogged and impossible to re-launch without gathering it all up, swimming back in, drying it out and starting again. And there was another issue concerning getting back upwind. Early kiteboarders spent a lot of time carrying their gear back from downwind runs, a combination of not yet having either the skill or the kind of kite or board that would make upwind runs possible.

The basic point was that, once again, activity was running ahead of product

development and people were using what kites were available rather than some specifically designed for the job. Ram air kites still have their supporters for water use to this day and in a light wind there's still very little to beat a big ram air kite. There are highly sophisticated dedicated water use ram airs available and they merit serious consideration for any would-be kiteboarder. In general wind conditions, however, there's another system that has swept all before it in both the competitive and commercial senses, filling the podium positions at nearly all the major kiteboarding events in the last few years.

In 1984, French brothers and master-mariners from Brittany, Bruno and Dominique Lagaignoux, patented a system for putting sealed inflatable tube stiffeners in a single skinned sail that could be flown as a kite on two lines attached directly to the wing's tips, the inflatable sections rendering it effectively unsinkable. Like all great ideas, it was very simple. The wing, though some way from the finished product, flew OK, pulled

hard enough for the resistance of rider on water, and was, technically speaking, fully water re-launchable. The inflatable tube stiffeners, one along the leading edge, and a series of vertical battens, have a dual function, providing both frame and buoyancy. The Legaignoux brothers always believed in the possibility of kiteboarding, trying many experiments themselves over the years without real success, but when pioneer kiteboarders like Manu Bertin saw the potential, they started using the kites. Within a couple of years inflatable kites had been fully adapted for kiteboarding and now command the entire market.

As the inflatable wing idea started to win converts and market share, so, crucially, other big windsurf manufacturers who were becoming aware of kiteboarding at that time, particularly opinion-formers like Robby Naish and Neil Pryde or Pete Cabrinha, decided that inflatable was the way to go, bought a license and started making kites. The rest, as they say, is history, as a huge list of manufacturers have followed the inflatable route in response to overwhelming competition success by, and consumer demand for, that type of kite, more than 90% of the total market for kiteboard kites.

Inflatable wings are very much the face of kiteboarding at present. Their tough build and the huge arched shape they take up in flight are very impressive and they really look the part. As the wing has stiffeners there's no need for complex bridles and it's back to the simplicity of flying lines attached directly to the wing tips. Although they rule the market presently there's no telling how things will look in a few years. Kiteboarding is a very young sport generally and is developing so fast that as far as the future is concerned, anything is possible.

Inflatable kites are increasingly sophisticated, which is not surprising with so many companies working on the same basic system, and many inflatables (leading-edge inflatables – LEIs – in tech speak) can now be used with either two or four lines. Almost all four-line water kites now have some kind of built-in de-power system, allowing you to adjust the pull while in motion by changing the angle of attack of the kite against the wind. Those that don't, soon will, because that's

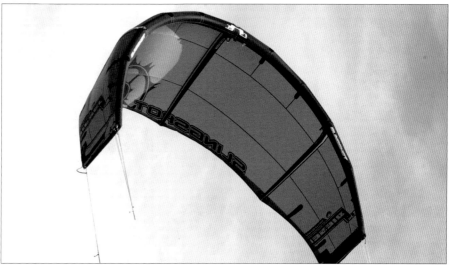

▶ *Top: Peter Lyn Guerilla, ram air waterkite*
▶ *Bottom: Slingshot inflatable bubble kite*

what the people want. The kites are designed to make getting back upwind easier and, needless to say, they exist in a huge range of sizes, tending to be somewhat larger in surface area than equivalent powered ram airs to compensate for their arched shape and the huge resistance of the small boards riders use nowadays against the water. Competition kites are very elongated; they have a very high aspect ratio giving them more power but making them more control sensitive. Beginner inflatable wings tend to have lower aspect ratios and be more rounded in shape, making them slower, more stable, and generally easier to handle. In this respect they conform exactly to the normal principles of kites.

So too with flying line control systems. It's a control bar world out there on the water now that they have been successfully adapted to take two-, four-, and even three-line set-ups incorporating de-power and quick release safety systems. In kiteboarding, there are far bigger kites and power involved in the equation, and harnesses are a must to be able to fly for any length of time, even at all. In the early days people used wind surf harnesses but now specific kite harnesses are being manufactured to deal with the different kind of loading and power kites give. Different length harness loops attached

> **When I first started kiting on the water in 1988 I knew it would be important to launch unassisted from any beach, boat or pier. My Kiteski and reelbar worked OK, but once inflatable kites came along and they worked so well I switched and never looked back. With all the refinements there've been since, I can get unbelievable performance out of my Phoenix kite in a huge range of conditions.**
>
> **CORY ROESELER Gaastra Kites Pro kiteboarder, kiteboard pioneer**

to the handles or control bar are used for different elements of riding and often carry independent safety quick release. Nevertheless, there are times when it's better to be unhooked, either for more mobility (for a "handle pass" move) or in case of getting into difficulties during a maneuver and being unable to unhook because of the pull of the kite.

We've already explored the technical details of ram air kites so don't propose to go over old ground here. Those companies still manufacturing ram air water kites have also responded to consumer pressure, their kites are even more efficient than before, have been able to incorporate principles such as de-power systems, and many of the water re-launch questions have also been answered. C-Quad kites too have been good performers and have played their part in the development of the sport. But, frustrat-

ingly for them both, it's a huge struggle for market share against the currently all-conquering arched inflatable kites.

Inflatable Bubble Kites

Being a big player in the kite industry is one thing. Competing with some of the heavyweights from the surf and windsurf industries is quite another. It's a potentially potent mix of past experiences, kites – boards – windsurf, coming together to drive the new sport forwards. All manufacturers have been forced to look to their strengths and the result has been a surge of acceleration in research and development of all kinds of product. Latterly, the industry has been obliged (by a relatively small – but occasionally fatal – number of accidents) to take a long, hard look at safety issues. It's true the industry probably wasn't prepared for the sudden growth there has been in the sport, but it has now well and truly caught up, and 2003 marked a watershed with every kite manufacturer developing and incorporating extra safety features. There's never been a better time to learn to kiteboard.

There's been a lot of confusion, since they were first licensed, about curved inflatable kite sizes (it's different with ram airs and Manta type, which are held flatter by their bridle structures), with different manufacturers using different, and quite legitimate, systems for measuring kite size. We're talking about the surface area of a wing kite, which, though flat when on the ground deflated, has a deeply arched curve when inflated ready for launch, and even more in flight. Although the inventors, the Legaignoux brothers, asked their licensees to end customer confusion by all working to the same system from 2002 onwards, that system being the projected area, there's still no industry standard. (Projected area is a calculation based on the sail area divided by a given factor. The other option is the flat area – the area of ground covered by the wing when laid

▶ *One of the original water men – Cory Roeseler*

flat on the ground.) It all makes for a highly confusing market, to say the least, especially for second-hand buyers. Make sure you know whether you're getting real or projected sail area when you buy and that it corresponds to what you actually want.

As for the construction, despite manufacturers' efforts to individualize their product, it's safe to say that the sail itself is generally made from tough ripstop polyester sailcloth, which is well known for its durability and low stretch. The inflatable tubes, bladders, or bubbles are made from polyurethane, and the pockets they fit into from durable polyester laminate. The kites are built for durability in extreme conditions and are usually heavily reinforced at all the wear and tear points, notably the leading edge, trailing edge, line attachments points, and wing tips. Design skills mean that all sizes of the same kite model have similar handling characteristics.

111

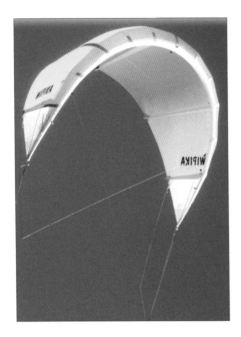

every inch of the sail studied to help maximize efficiency and reduce drag. They're the product of at least five years of progress, designed and built specifically for kiteboarding at its most efficient as the sport stands today and almost certainly for some time to come, as there's no sign yet of a convincing alternative to inflatable kites as a water option. No wonder then that there are new manufacturers appearing every year. There are already too many to list here and, anyway, imagine if we left anyone out... Use the net, buy a magazine, check the ads, visit the sites or shops, go to an event – there's a bewildering array of equipment out there to tempt you, and until you start looking you won't know what you want.

Two-and Four-line Kites: The Big Difference

We mentioned that some water kites are convertible from four control lines to two, or vice versa. Some are only available as a two-line model. There are some major differences between the two that merit an explanation.

One major difference is that flying on two lines only means not having the bene-

fit of a de-power system. If you hook into your harness while flying on a control bar you'll be at full power, depending on the kite's position in the wind window. And if you don't hook into your harness you'll be at full power but carrying all the weight on your arms. Another is in the kite speed. Generally speaking two-line kites are faster through the air and more mobile. They've got less line drag (obviously) and there are no brake lines; the kite's profile can't be altered.

People who've traditionally liked the speed and raw power of a two-line set-up have been wakeboarders and wake-style riders who tend to do their tricks lower down to the water than the freestyle big air merchants and wave riders who find the mobility of the kite well suited to the need to generate power quickly when negotiating the water contours. Four-line riders will argue in favor of the extra control over the kite, plus the reassurance and technical advantage they gain from their de-power systems. Certainly, launching and landing a big two-line kite is fraught with risk because of the reduced control you have at what is a critical phase, and it shouldn't be attempted without a helper.

The fact is that many kiteboard schools take you though a two-line phase before you start dealing with the extra pair of

Flying lines attach directly to the sail tips, but multiple front and rear control-line attachment point options (knot-head toggles) make it possible to tune the kite to different styles or conditions, more or less power, faster or slower flying speed. The system linking the battens to the leading edge gives the kite a solid frame, enabling faster turns and providing improved stability. The kites are designed to ride out wind turbulence and gusts,

▲ *The original: An early Wipika inflatable kite*

lines and the de-power system. That's another argument two-line flyers will make: you have to be a better pilot, the kites are less forgiving, and that makes you safer, you can't rely on something you haven't got to get you out of trouble. Saying that, the vast majority of riders nowadays are opting for four lines. It's also true that if you're used to a conventional two- or four-line kite, then flying a bubble kite on four lines with that de-power system working changes the whole nature of how you handle the kite, in one very important way.

With a conventional kite, if you want to generate more power or get the kite to climb, you pull back with your arms and walk backwards on the ground. Forget all that. With a de-power system hooked onto your harness and fully operational, to get the kite to climb, you push forward with your arms, opening the trailing edge, de-powering the kite but enabling it to generate lift from the airflow across its surface. It makes many aspects of handling the kite different and makes it vitally important that you fully familiarize yourself with the kite and de-power system on land before you go anywhere near water. It goes against everything you've learned before and you may need a little un-learning of old habits as much as learning of new ones.

Kiteboards

The First Kiteboards

In the beginning of kiteboarding the kites were lacking a little and took time to adapt, and the boards didn't exist at all. Most early kiteboarding efforts were made on home-adapted surf or windsurf boards or water skis. All used some kind of foot bindings (like on a windsurf board), essential for working against the pull of the kites. These DIY boards were all right to get the sport up and running but weren't designed for the specific strains and loading of kiteboarding, specially when it came to the question of jumping and, in particular, the landings after jumps.

Of course it didn't take long for shapers and manufacturers from within the established sports of surf, wakeboard, and windsurf, (specially the last), to start to look seriously at the new sport, and kite specific boards soon started to appear, reinforced for kite power. With its obvious link to windsurfing, most early kiteboards conformed to the directional principle. That is to say, they were made to go in one direction only. They were classic boards with plenty of volume to keep you afloat and a three-fin (thruster) configuration at the rear for stability, course holding and control. Being mono-directional

> **Everyone is allowed their own opinion on the subject of boards, that's one of the unique and awesome things about kiteboarding. A friend of mine had no money so he took a chunk of plywood, put foot straps on it and it worked fine, he could go upwind and everything. Then one day he had a go on my Naish production mutant board and I never saw it again! A real kiteboard is a real kiteboard, you can ride anything!**
>
> **ADAM KOCH Naish Kites international team pro kiteboarder**

(forwards only) meant that they had to be turned round for you to get back to your start point, the objective being to go backwards and forwards across the wind, even upwind, skill level, board, kite, and conditions allowing. Jibing was as much part of the essential requirement as beach starting, water re-launching, and getting up on the board at all – mainly because the only alternative to jibing was to stop, put the kite at the zenith, take the board off and turn it to point the other way, then water-start again.

Just as some kiteboarders came to the sport from windsurfing, so others had had prior experience of wakeboarding and snowboarding. Wakeboards are generally short and very thin; the rider is strapped into full-foot bindings, like on a snowboard, and towed behind a power boat, playing and tricking on the boat's wake. Snowboards are longer, more flex-ible and able to go in both directions. It didn't take wakeboarders long to realize that you could use the same board with a big kite for power. You could even use a similar control bar to steer the kite and the standard 15-minute pay-per-tow has become a session as long as there's wind available. Wakeboards made for a much "trickier" style of riding. As they were much shorter and less voluminous, riders needed to be super powered-up to stay afloat. Wakeboards, like snow-boards, are also normally symmetrical lengthways, having fins at both ends to allow riders to lead with either foot during trick sessions. The implication for kiteboarding was immense: if the board could lead in either direction, there wouldn't be any need to turn around. To go back the other way you simply reverse your direction. The downside is that being so small, fast, and radical,

and needing as much wing power as they do, wakeboards are not really suitable for beginners. Also, being permanently strapped in to your foot bindings can make life a bit scary if you do get into difficulties.

What was required was a symmetrical board with sufficient volume for stability and fins at both ends for reversability. The boards duly started to appear during late 2000, The first symmetrical dedicated kiteboards were developed by top French rider Franz Olry during 2001 and 2002. Twin tip mania was born. Kiteboarding had finally established its individuality and differentness from windsurfing, because you can't twin tip a windsurf board. With kite power, you want to turn around? You slow the board down almost to a stop and quickly, before it can sink, shift your weight and get the wing and the board going in the opposite direction. Better still, a quick jump and transition... You can still turn around if you want and ride on the other, frontside, edge for your return, but then you'll be flying over your shoulder with your back to the kite. In surf sports, frontside is what's in front of your toes and backside is what's behind your heels.

▶ Top: Early directional kiteboards
▶ Bottom: Gaastra symmetrical twin tips

How Kiteboards Have Developed

As a result of the improvements in design and construction of boards and kites over the years, it's perfectly possible to learn kitesurfing on a twin tip, without having to learn the jibe, and not surprisingly this is overwhelmingly the most popular type of board in the world today. But the sport is constantly developing and recent experiments have seen the appearance of WakeSkate boards – a small, tricky, no-straps board, mini directionals, mutants, plus specialized boards for big wave, speed, and distance kiteboarding, some of which are going back to a more directional shape and taking the foot straps off again!

Kiteboarding can genuinely claim to be a highly successful fusion of other sports and nowhere is this reflected more than in board shaping and design. But the basic kiteboarding family remains directionals, wakeboards, and twin tips. The general principle is: big board, small wind; small board, big wind. A big volume board in a big wind is just too much to handle, and a small board in a small wind might well sink because it hasn't got the flotation or

power to keep it up. Mini twin tips and wakeboards are all the rage with experienced riders, and new mini directionals are giving the old format a new lease on life. Mini boards are great for fast action on the water and trickery in the air, giving rise to a radical skateboard style with lots of grabbed "one-foots" and "no-foots" – jumping and holding the board, taking one or both feet out of the straps and back in again before landing (that kind of thing is not possible on a wakeboard because your feet are strapped in). Handle passes, however, came from wakeboarding and have superseded one or no-foot moves as the benchmark of riding excellence. With such a small board you need loads of kite power to keep you going, so most riders are very powered-up. This is another reason why they're not a great choice for beginners. The other general board principle is that you should learn on a bigger volume board that will be slower, more stable and keep you afloat better. That means wait for light to moderate winds, too. Small boards and big winds are not for beginners.

With the change in style of boards has come a change in style of riding too. Where the big volume directionals are great for planing, small twin tips and especially wakeboards are ridden much more aggressively on the edges. Competition riding,

▶ *Franz Olry: Genius rider and inventor of the twin tip concept*

which is the inspiration for so much of the media coverage and public interest, exists in four main formats, at least on the major tours and event circuit:

- **freestyle – free riding with the emphasis on tricks and fluid riding, aerial gymnastics, transitions, and variety of moves; includes rotations, grabs, board-off moves, handle passes, and so on**
- **hang time – who can stay up in the air longest (not necessarily the biggest jump)**
- **wave riding – a more surf style of riding that aims to exploit the wave's contours to execute moves such as off-the-lips and bottoms, and getting in the famous "tube"**
- **kitespeed – the fastest rider over a measured distance, trying to beat windsurfers and sailors to be the first sail-powered entity to break the 50-knot barrier.**

Board shaping for kites is now big business, and most of the big surf and windsurf manufacturers have ranges of dedicated kiteboards distinct from their other products. There are also special ranges of fins, which play such a vital role in controlling the board. Board evolution is far from complete; on the contrary, in many ways it's only just beginning and there's talk of new revolutionary shapes that enable you to ride with no side slide. With a sport that's so young, and a speed

of development so rapid, anything is possible. There are dozens of manufactures and dozens more customboard shapers out there aiming to make it so.

You'll be faced with another bewildering choice if you start looking around at the number of different board models on the market, which is another reason why it's a good idea to go to a kiteboard school. That way you can not only test out one or two models, you can build up a much better picture of your level and what kind of board is best adapted to your needs while you learn and before you spend your money. Go to the spots and talk to the riders, ask their advice. Do a little techno surfing on the internet where there's a vast amount of manufacturer and rider information available. Don't be suckered into buying equipment – board or kite – that's beyond your skill level; you'll just have a hard time and risk killing your interest off for life. You can always trade up later or keep the original to lend to a friend to help them get started.

Inflatable Kites

Setting Up
These are serious "toys" and come in a serious package. Normally that means a heavy-duty, breathable, custom storage bag with a logo. It's good enough to withstand the worst that airline baggage handlers can do to them with the kite fully packed down as it came from the factory. The bag is normally adjustable so you carry your kite in a temporary pack-down state, leading edge deflated but battens inflated. It's not recommended that you leave your battens inflated any length of time (no more than overnight).

Not all "extras" packages are the same – they vary from brand to brand – but at the very least you should expect to find inside the carry bag is a high-debit pump for inflating the leading edge and battens, an ergonomic control bar fitted with a de-power and safety systems, a pre-stretched color-coded quad flying line, set appropriately for the size of kite you're buying, a kite repair kit for running repairs, and a full instruction manual. If for any reason any of this equipment is not in the bag you should contact your dealer or the manufacturer directly. Try to remember, as you unroll the sail for the first time, how it was rolled to leave the factory so that you can roll it back the same way when you pack it away each time. You may want to try this once at home but you're going to need to know the full procedure for when you get out on the beach, lake, or riverside. Take a look at the diagram opposite, which will help make sense of it all. Memorize and follow your step-by-step preparation instructions to the letter.

If this was the start of a boarding session, now would be the moment to stop and put on your final pieces of safety equipment: crash helmet, harness, and buoyancy or flotation aid. You might want to get used to this anyway while you're learning to fly the kite, as that's the way it's going to be when you come to do it for real. To begin with, though, get used to flying it without your harness until you've fully understood basic control. It's a completely different experience flying a big kite with your movement restricted by your wetsuit, harness, and so on. Specially built kiteboarding wetsuits and harnesses are now produced and these are designed with the extra flexibility of the articulations required by kiteboarders in mind.

The next stage will be to unwind your flying lines. Riders tend to use lines between 75 and 120 feet, longer in light to moderate wind and shorter lines (60 feet) in strong wind. There's a new trend towards even shorter lines – as short as 45 feeet – which could help fit more riders into the same space of water. As you will be learning in light to moderate winds your lines should be at the longer end of the range. The lines must be the

Setting up an inflatable wing

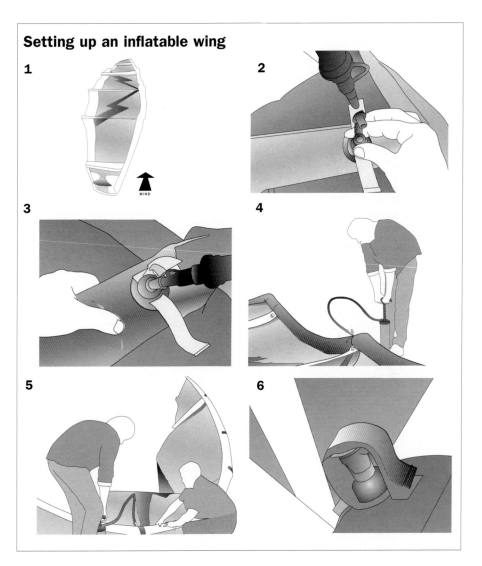

appropriate strength for the size of your kite in its maximum wind, taking into account that when you use a kite on water there is about 30 per cent more strain on the flying lines than when flying on land. This is due to the extra resistance of the water against your board and body. In fact your lines will be made of high-quality Spectra (Dyneema), with their advantages of low stretch, low weight, low diameter (in relation to equivalent strength nylon or polyester), and good slipperiness. Unlike your ram air traction kites, the lines will be of equal strength as the loadings are more evenly distributed between front and back. They will be sleeved at each end to prevent snapping where knots are tied; Spectra (Dyneema) has a low melting point so friction from knots would cause the lines to cut through themselves at the knot. This sleeving will be color coded to help you easily identify the left and right, and the line attachment points on the kite are also color coded to prevent incorrect attachment. Similarly, there is a loop and toggle system for your lark's head knot, set up in such a way that you can only attach the lines in the correct manner, no mistakes possible.

► Cabrinha hand pump with retaining leash

Attach the loose ends as instructed using the lark's head knot. You're ready to start unwinding the lines, which will normally come pre-wound onto and attached to your control bar. Unwind them fully as described in the kite or wing instruction manual. Give them a thorough final check to make sure they're correctly attached – launching with your lines incorrectly attached can risk serious injury to you and others. And there's another safety issue you'll need to deal with at this moment: almost all makes of water kite now come with a kite leash fitted as standard as part of their safety equipment. We'll talk about that more in the section on safety later in this chapter, but whatever safety leash system you have should be attached now. Ready? I think you probably are...

Launching

Kiteboarding kites develop immense power and must be treated with respect. This is never more the case than during the launch and land phases, when the kite is not yet in, or is just leaving, full pilot control. There is a safe way of solo launching in lighter winds, especially now that manufacturers are really turning their attention to their safety features. The safe way applies to a standard kite as much as to one fitted with a special solo launch device. If your kite is fitted with a solo launch device you will need to familiarize yourself fully with its functioning, which may make certain phases of the launch or landing sequence different from those described here. Always check with your dealer or the manufacturer if you are in any doubt. For maximum safety it's recommended that you always use an assisted launch, preferably from another kiteboarder. The assisted launch is advised because until and even when you're used to handling the kite there's a chance you could get into difficulties. In big winds, and with big kite sizes, it's recommended, however much experience you've got, to use the assisted launch. But you're probably busting to know about solo launching so let's take a look at that first.

Let's assume you're in position and so is the kite – on its back at about 45 degrees to window center, leading edge facing the edge of the wind window. Then:

1 Take a couple of paces backwards, pulling smoothly, gently and evenly on the control bar. As you do so, tension will come onto the downwind tip lines, making the tip rise off the ground, and you will feel pressure beginning to build in the sail.

2 Keep moving gently backwards and the downwind tip will rise further. Then tension will come onto the upwind tip and lines,

Solo Launching

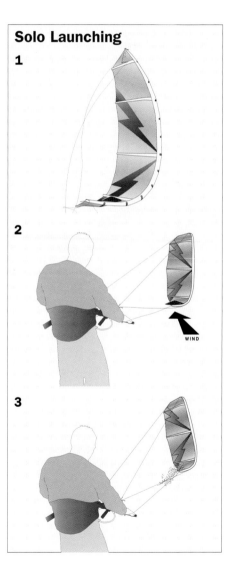

1

2

WIND

3

pulling it towards you. As it does so it will unfold and dump its load of sand on the ground. If you don't fold the wing tip over there's a chance the sand won't be removed and it may foul your launch. Hold the bar diagonally in the same plane as the kite to help maintain its position facing the edge of the wind window. You will now feel considerably more pressure on the lines as the kite sail fills with wind.

3 Once the kite has got rid of its sand it will lift itself off the ground and, as long as you keep even pressure on the flying lines, will fly to a "safe" position on the edge of the wind window.

From here you can steer it up the wind window, pulling gently on the upper tip and lines, until it reaches the zenith, above your head. Neutralize your steering to stabilize the kite there.

1 For an assisted launch, make sure you brief your caddy before you start. There's no difference in the positioning of kite or flyer unless you're in a strong wind, in which case set the kite up closer to the edge of the window. The caddy should stand downwind, behind the kite.

2 When you're ready to launch, as you start to move backwards and pull gently on the control bar, the caddy should hold the downwind tip of the kite up to the wind and, as it lifts up, hold the leading

121

edge of the wing to stabilize it during this phase.

3 With the kite full of wind and ready to go, the caddy should hold it by the center of the leading edge, from where there are two options: on your launch, signal that the caddy can release it, take a few steps backwards to get out of the way, and let you fly the kite to safety; alternatively, if you signal to abort the launch, the caddy must grab the kite quickly, turn it on its back to de-power it, and immobilize it again. What you must do is agree your signals. Try using hand or arm signals, because the noise of wind and water can make it difficult to communicate orally. It's also important for the caddy to release the kite simply at the appropriate moment, not to try and throw it. Once the kite is out of the caddy's hands you follow the normal procedure for steering it up to the zenith.

Assisted Launch

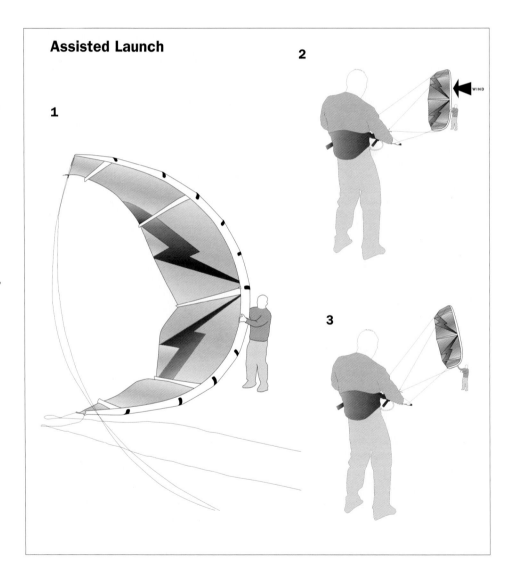

1

2

WIND

3

Steering

With the kite stable at the zenith, this is the moment when, if this was a kite-boarding session, you would hook into your harness and get your board leash fastened ready to hit the water. During your first few sessions, while you are learning the flying controls, you are advised not to hook in. You need to know how to fly the kite confidently before adding new dimensions such as the harness.

At this stage your only way of controlling (as in reducing) power is to move forwards or steer the wing further out of the window. It's going to be a good workout because you'll be dealing with the full power of the kite with your arms, then your body, rather than the other way around. Try moving the kite backwards and forwards across the top of the wind window at first. The steering is very similar to a two-line kite, even when flying with four control lines. Many or most kite schools require you to fly a two-line inflatable before moving on to a four line with de-power system. To steer:

■ **Pull back gently but firmly on the right side of the control bar, at the same time pushing forward with the left, until you see**

▶ *Make sure you have fully mastered controlling the kite on land before hitting the water*

the kite start to turn to the right. As soon as it's pointing slightly to the right, neutralize your steering to let it fly in that direction. It may descend slightly as it does so.

■ Before it reaches the edge of the window, pull gently but firmly back on the left end of the control bar until you see the kite turn to face slightly left. Neutralize your steering to let it fly back across the top of the window. It will probably rise a little towards center window and fall again as it moves slightly left. Don't forget, the wind window is curved.

■ Before it reaches the left edge of the window pull back again on the right side and so on. You can stabilize the kite at the zenith by turning it to point straight up as you reach window center.

Once you've done that a few times it's time to try some full loops; this will get you skidding and be good practice for the body-dragging stage you'll be going through before getting onto your board. The idea will be to make a horizontal figure eight again, but this time bringing the kite down through the power zone to initiate the sequence before turning up at the edge and down through the middle again. The kite will power up big time as it dives but that's what you're going to need to do to get your kiteboard going on the water. To manage that power:

- With the kite stable at the zenith, pull back gently on the right tip of the control bar, pushing forward with the left also. This will move the kite to the right of the top of the window.
- Now pull back hard on the left side of the control bar, pushing forward on the right, to dive the kite down and left until it's pointing almost (but not quite) vertically downwards, through the center of the wind window. It will power up hard and fast so brace yourself, lean back, hold on, and enjoy the buzz...
- With the power maxing and the kite accelerating downwards, you'll be sliding forwards. Now firmly, but not too suddenly, reverse your steering, pulling back hard on the right side of the control bar. The kite will pull out of its dive and begin climbing up the left-hand side of the wind window, making a big loop. At this point the kite will be losing power but gaining in lift as it climbs. If you ended up lying down, now's the time to use that lift to stand up again.
- Keep your steering on until the kite comes around full circle and is pointing almost vertically down the wind towards the right-hand side, where the whole process starts again: the power kicks in as the kite dives, pull on the left side of the bar to bring the kite up out of its dive, loop up the right side of the wind window, over the top and down the middle again.
- At this point your lines are untwisted again. Technically it doesn't matter but it's much better not to fly with twists – excessive twists and big power could cause the lines to lock resulting in considerable risk.

Once you are confident about making the right and left loop, you can fly around and explore the wind window, feeling the pull in different positions in the window. Standing on the ground you will feel good, continuous pull doing a flat figure eight (successive left and right loops) in the sky. Once you get out on the water, there's another kind of maneuver you will need to know for the occasions when you need to work the kite if the wind is light for the size of kite you're flying, which is often the case when you're learning. It's a kind of S pattern on its side, or sinusoidal, that you fly near the edge of the wind window; it keeps powering the kite up as you move it around, similar to the horizontal figure eight:

- With the kite stable at the zenith, pull back firmly but gently on the right end of your control bar to turn it to the right. Keep turning it until it's pointing downwards at 45 degrees. As it comes down the side of the wind window it will begin to power up and accelerate.
- As the kite reaches a 45-degree angle to the ground, pull back firmly on the left end of your control bar, turning it up at 45 degrees again (a 90 degree turn). Keep the steering on and turn the kite so that it climbs up the wind window.
- Before it slows down and loses power, pull on the right end of your control bar again to turn the kite through 90 degrees to the right and down again, where it will power up once more and accelerate towards the ground or water as before.
- At this point you can keep the kite moving in a continuous pattern, working it up and down the edge of the wind window to try gain power. The lower the kite comes in the sky the more lateral pull there will be and the more you will be able to work your board's edges.

Landing

As with the launch, the landing is a potentially hazardous moment and your landings should always be made with a helper or caddy. Other than if using a special solo launch or land device, it is not possible to land solo (alone) and it should not be attempted. If you are using a solo landing device, please refer to the manufacturer's instructions and make sure you familiarize yourself with its functioning in light winds fully before attempting to fly in stronger winds.

First of all you must have a big enough landing area, preferably away from other site users. If you are in a group of kiteboarders you must agree where your landing and launching area is before starting and always head for that place when you want to get off your board and land the kite. You need to have your caddy correctly positioned between 75 and 120 feet downwind of you (depending on your line length) at the edge of the wind window; the caddy should approach the kite from behind, downwind, as you fly it close to the ground. Then:

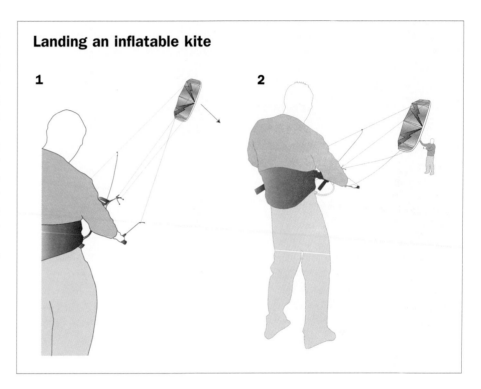

Landing an inflatable kite

1

2

- With the kite at the zenith, pull gently on the right end of your control bar and turn the kite to the right. Don't pull it into a full loop: steer it gently but steadily down the edge of the wind window, keeping the leading edge pointing towards the edge of the wind window, never straight down.
- As the kite approaches ground level, maneuver yourself on the ground so you can fly it close to your caddy. Keep flying

out towards the edge of the window so there's minimum power.
- Your caddy should position themselves so they can approach the kite from downwind, behind it. When your caddy can reach the center of the leading edge they should grab it, turn the kite on its back and be ready to walk it to a safe position to immobilize it.
- You can now detach your safety leash and walk the kite to a safe position. Place it

face down, leading edge pointing into the wind, and weight the leading edge down with sand to immobilize it.

As with the launch, you should not make a landing when you are hooked on to your harness. If you start with the kite at the zenith and fly it down the edge of the window it should have minimum power as it descends.

> **" A de-power strap is hugely important to the sport of kiteboarding. If the wind was perfect everywhere you wouldn't need it, but when the wind is always changing your de-power strap allows you to adjust the power your kite is producing. As the wind gets stronger you can sheet out like a sailboat or windsurfer can do, you can kiteboard over-powered but still in control. "**
>
> **MARK DOYLE Slingshot International Team pro kiteboarder**

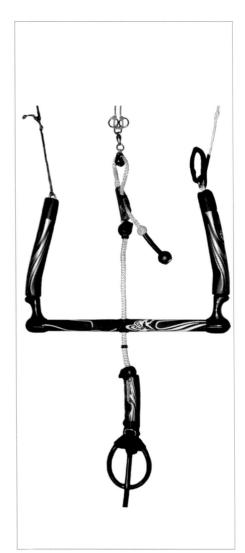

The De-power System

De-power systems have helped popularize kiteboarding, making it much easier to learn, in the same way that four-line control of ram airs did buggying ten years ago. There are almost as many variants to the basic principle of de-power systems as there are manufacturers – they all do it slightly differently. What we'll explain here is the basic principle; it's up to each and every kiteboarder to understand his or her own system through full reading of the instructions and a period of training to adjust to how it works and affects the kite.

If you're flying a four-line kite, as many people are nowadays, it's almost certainly fitted with a highly effective power control system that is simple to

▶ *Slingshot control bar showing the sliding center line de-power system and quick-release safety toggle*

operate. It's linked to your harness and control bar and, once you start flying hooked into your harness, you will find things very different but relatively easy to adjust to and wonder how life ever functioned normally beforehand. Using the de-power system you can fly with your harness on, so make sure you have fully learned to fly the kite without the harness before you move on to this stage.

On the control bar there are usually (not always) two harness loops, or strops, in the center. These are heavy-duty vinyl-coated loops. The longer one is attached directly to the bar. This is called the power strop and once you hook into this you are committed to full-on power until you unhook again, as with a two-line kite. The other, de-power, loop is fitted onto the end of the leader line for the kite's front lines, which passes through a hole or a fitting at the center of the control

bar. This is commonly known as the "chicken" loop, the inference being that if you need to de-power you must be chicken. (Not exactly the safety attitude the sport needs.) Further along this leader line towards the line attachments there is a "stop" fixed in position. Once you are hooked into the short harness loop, you can regulate the power by pushing the bar away from you evenly with both hands. With the front lines fixed to your harness, this has the effect of pushing the rear lines away, breaking the profile of the trailing edge, changing the angle of attack, spilling some of the kite's wind, and losing power. Not only is there a stop, there's a second level of power tuning on most kites, usually a locking adjustment for the range of de-power you can obtain. Some of them allow you to make adjustments while riding. Check these in your instructions and ask your dealer for advice. It's impossible to explain all the different variants of the locking system here – every manufacturer tries to individualize their kite with these kinds of gizmos. It's important that you understand fully how yours works before you power up fully or go on the water, but once you do you will be able to choose your own settings anywhere between the two extremes.

With skill and practice you will be able to fine tune the power at various points of your kiteboarding activity, for instance powering up for jumps, to tweak some extra out of what you're doing. Equally valuably, de-power systems enable you to deal with big gusts and squalls out on the water, limiting the power surge, and hopefully giving you the breathing space you need to ride it out and wait for the power to drop again. In fact, any time you feel that the power is too much and you're hooked into your de-power loop, you can use it in this way.

You can usually take it a step further, too. If you let go of the bar altogether it will slide along the leader line until it meets the "stop." This releases the rear lines and keeps the front lines pulled. What normally happens is that the kite almost completely de-powers and flies itself to the edge or top of the wind window, where you can recover it. Get plenty of practice on dry land with your de-power system, trying it in every conceivable circumstance, before you find yourself trying to work out how to do it out on the water.

Please be aware that, if you're flying a four-line ram air wing on handles or a two-

◀ *Cabrinha control bar in action. Push away to de-power and pull in (as shown here) to power up*

127

❝ **In the past, pro riders stopped using safety leashes because it interfered with their riding styles, but with lots of well-publicized accident injuries and even fatalities we have all seen the consequences of not using proper safety equipment. Leashes are more rider-friendly now and the only excuse for not using a safety system nowadays is that you bought your stuff used or from a brand that cares more about having your money than saving your life.** ❞

CORY ROESELER Gaastra Kites pro kiteboarder, kiteboard pioneer

line wing on a control bar, you will not have an effective de-power system. In the former scenario you will have the handles to make adjustments to the angle of attack of the wing and, if it all gets to be too much, a wrist leash for safety (see below). A two-line control bar usually has either a leash safety system or in some cases is fitted with a third line coming from the center rear of the wing, attached to the center of the bar on a leader with a stop. Letting go of the bar pulls on the third line, applying maximum brakes and de-powering the kite, causing it to sink to the ground or water.

The Safety System

Kiteboarding being the dangerous activity that it is, safety very quickly became an issue. Some kind of safety system was needed that would allow you to let go of the control bar or handles to de-power the wing totally but stay attached to it so you could recover it afterwards. Even after the de-power system, riders still felt in need of some kind of ultimate, instant way out, especially for those moments when you're not hooked onto your de-power loop. The simplest solution requires a leash running from your wrist or harness to one of the (rear) lines. If you then let go of your bar when not hooked in, or action your quick release, the control bar is released and the kite retained by one rear line only, neutralizing its power almost instantaneously and causing it to sink to the ground or water. The problem is that for advanced-level riders who are doing jumps and transitions that involve full rotations, the leash gets in the way, impedes mobility, and can foul rider, flying lines, or board. Many

manufacturers have been working towards leash-free but safe systems for retaining the kite. This has become particularly important since many riders try to nail the handle pass move, which entails passing the bar from one hand to the other, behind your back, up in the air.

Often nowadays there's a safety system quick release on the chicken loop and you'll need to be hooked into this to be able to make full use of the control bar's safety features. As a first step you can let go of the control bar completely; it will then slide up to its stop point and de-power the kite. If this is not sufficient, action your quick release. At this point you will no longer be able to consider re-launching as, once actioned, the quick release must be properly re-set. You'll need to follow the full back-to-shore procedure and re-set it on land before you can ride again. Normally, if you're not wearing a kite leash, this is your ultimate sanction and might be needed if, for instance, a kite you've already let go of at this stage is then snagged by a boat propeller on water or a chair lift on snow. Up to this point you are still attached to the kite and can recover it for the swim back without too much trouble. Actioning this ultimate safety system completely detaches you from the kite and really

An example of a safety system

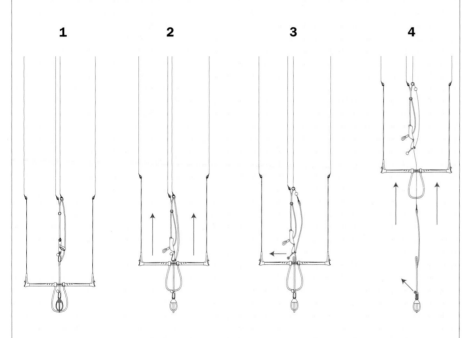

1   2   3   4

1 To use the safety system you must have the chicken loop attached to your harness.

2 Letting go of your bar will cause the kite to de-power.

3 Pull the quick-release toggle to release the bar and control systems.

4 All power will be released from the kite. The control systems will slide along the center leash system towards the kite and you may have to pull the safety release on the chicken loop.

should be used only in the most extreme circumstances. You are safely away from trouble but your released kite now represents a danger to other kiteboarders or site users. Now you will have to hope that your kite blows to shore nearby or that someone else helps you recover it in a boat. What better reasons could there be always to use a kite leash?

It's vitally important that you are completely familiar with all the safety procedures before you go out on a board, including re-setting them. The system is only as good as the person operating it and if he or she hasn't practiced... It is even worth practicing recovering your bar in shallow water before you have to do it for real out of your depth.

Learn Kiteboarding From An Accredited Teacher Or School

It goes without saying that what you're about to do is highly dangerous. Not only is there the immense power of the kite, there are the hard edges of the board that can hurt and then there's the small matter of the water, drowning, being lost at sea, and so on. In circumstances such as those, as a complete beginner, by far the best thing you can do is go and take a series of lessons at an accredited school. That way, you get the right sort of advice and training in a secure environment with rescue boats, full insurance and all the other creature comforts that make learning easier. You can test out equipment before you buy (assuming you haven't already) and see if you actually think you've got the endurance to get through the learning phase. Everybody says that, as a complete beginner, you've got to expect to drink a lot of water during your first few sessions. But everybody also says that there's nothing like the experience of your first success in getting up on a kiteboard.

Whether you've come from a boarding background or a kiting background, lessons will still be a good idea as there's at least 50 per cent of the package you know little or nothing about at this stage.

Accredited by whom exactly? The whole sport has come as something of a surprise and a lot of its growth and history have been pretty anarchic. Some countries have a national body overseeing their sport, and how that functions varies enormously depending on which country you're in.

In the US there are numerous regional or local clubs and associations, too many to begin to list here. There's also an organization that, similarly to the French FFVL, is trying to co-ordinate and promote safe practice in various wind sports on a national level. It is the Professional Air Sports Association (PASA), dedicated to "promoting and preserving the air sports industry" and able to "offer information on the industry of Hang Gliding, Kiteboarding, Paragliding, Parasailing and Ultra Light Flying for individuals and businesses". It is working on national standard certification for schools and instructors, runs instructor courses, and offers insurance plus advice on best or safe practice.

Membership of sports bodies usually costs relatively little (compared with the equipment) and, importantly, includes insurance, which makes it a great investment. You might well find classes available via your local kite or windsurf dealer, at a wind- or water-sports center, marina, beach windsurf school or similar. Check that they are properly accredited before you book. There's one worldwide body that has a similar function, instructs instructors, approves courses and issues test standards for equipment. It's called the International Kiteboarding Organisation (IKO). The IKO is sponsored by a number of big name manufacturers as a means of bringing newcomers into the sport safely, and promoting and co-ordinating the safe development of the sport.

A good kiteboard school will have classes for different skill levels of rider. Be honest about your skill level when choosing your course. Courses are structured to deal with your skill level and progression and, like all sports, you need to understand the basics first and foremost. If you can, check out the site too in advance. The best possible conditions for learning are somewhere with plenty of space, flat water, and smooth wind, but also water that is shallow over a large area. While you are learning you are going to spend a lot of time falling in the water and re-starting. Somewhere with good, shallow "lagoon" water will make the process of getting back in position to re-start much, much easier and save you a lot of drinking time, in both senses.

Starting Up And Riding

Once you've got your kite launched there are two distinct stages to starting up. The first is getting the kite hooked onto your harness and you attached to the board, then taking the whole ensemble to the water. The second stage is actually getting up and riding on the board. This assumes

" The best way to start up is get out there and do it. The sport is not that hard to learn and you will find it very exciting on the first day. "

MARK DOYLE Slingshot International Team pro kiteboarder

that you're a beginner rider and that you're going to be using a large-volume directional or twin tip for learning, and that it's fitted with foot straps. There's a completely different option for anyone who's riding with full-foot bindings, because obviously you can't walk to the water when you're strapped onto a board. You've got to set up near the water's edge or just in the water and perform a beach start. And you are going to need a caddy (helper) to fly the kite while you strap yourself into your bindings and give the control bar to you when you're ready to go. Riding with full-foot bindings is an advanced technique, one that you can learn once you are confident about the kiteboarding basics.

You're going to need good conditions to help you learn. In kiteboarding terms that means anything from about 8 to 15 knots of wind speed. Anything more than that and things can start to get a bit strong. Anything less and you won't get up on the board. Another factor you must consider is wind direction. Offshore wind is to be avoided at all costs. Apart from being very lumpy and gusty if it's coming off the land, making everything difficult,

it will blow you out to the open sea and maximum danger. Pay full respect to the elements and they won't mistreat you. An onshore wind, while almost certainly smooth, will tend to blow you onto the beach as you inevitably travel more downwind at first, and make it difficult even getting out past the beach or shore break of the waves. The best winds are sideshore, blowing along the beach, or cross-on, blowing diagonally onto the beach. These two allow you, if you're able to tack or reach across the wind successfully, to run out from the beach and back in again, better still getting back upwind. Once you can get back upwind you can afford to start trying some jumps, knowing that you can regain all the distance lost downwind in the air during your jump. The better your skill level and the more competent and confident you are, the further you'll be able to go from your start point. You should never, under any circumstances ride out of sight of land.

When you're sure that conditions are good and you've made all your preparations:

1 Launch the kite on the edge of the wind window and steer it carefully up to the zenith. Now hook into your harness. This should be on the short loop, the one attached to your safety or de-power system. With this in place you can activate it if you get into difficulties. At this point you should be able to control the kite with one hand, keeping it stable in the minimum power position at the zenith, pushing or pulling on one end of the bar.

2/3 Having established total control over the kite, it's time to attend to the other half of the equation, the board. Locate your board and, keeping one hand and one eye on controlling the wing, attach your board leash to your ankle with your free hand. Keeping the kite at the zenith, pick up the board with your free hand, tuck it under your arm and make your way carefully to the water, walking far enough out for you and the board to be able to float, but not so far that you can't touch the bottom.

So far so good. If your kite skills are good enough you'll be able to get in and out of the water with ease. Practice that sequence until you're completely comfortable with the whole process. What comes next is more difficult in the sense that now you'll be multi-functioning again, between kite and board. But now after sufficient years of kiteboarding experience

131

and development, equipment is designed towards your succeeding. Be confident, go for it – you'll be amazed how easy it is once you've got it.

Water Start

To prepare for your water start you will need to have the board in front or downwind of you. Try going to your good side first (everyone has a good and bad side to begin with). It's easier to move the board than yourself so bring the board in front of you so that you're facing it. Hold the board by its rear strap as it will be easier to maneuver. Then:

- Position the board so it's pointing across and slightly downwind, and tilt it at an angle so that you can easily get your feet into the straps. Start with your front or lead foot, then the rear, sitting down in the water if necessary. As you put your front foot in, if the kite starts to power up again pull slightly with your front hand and press the board with your front foot a little to adjust your position rather than overbalance and have to start all over again.
- This is the most awkward moment, lying on your back, feet in the straps, no power in the kite and waves washing over your face. Steer the kite across the top of the wind window, to the "rear" window,

Attaching your board leash

1

2

3

Water Start

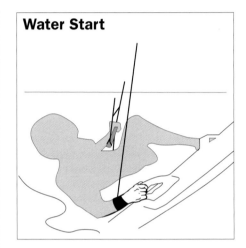

opposite to the direction you want to go in. Be careful not to let it go too far behind.

- Now steer the kite back across the wind window towards the side you want to move towards, diving the kite down into the window as you do so to power it up. Be careful not to bring the wing too low or it will pull you forwards before you are ready. Keep your knees bent and lean back to lever against the power.
- As you feel yourself being pulled forwards, brace your legs to wedge the flat of the board against the water. Steer the kite up the edge of the wind window. Keep your legs braced and let the kite pull you gradually up on the board as it climbs the wind window. In lighter winds you may need to use the S pattern to build power up. Strong or light,

you will need to press with your rear heel to dig the rear edge in and aim the board back upwind. Then press more with your front foot once up and planing to hold your course.

■ If the wind's good enough you can lock the kite in position on the edge of the wind window. Keep your body flexed and work the board with your feet. It's all in the feet at this stage – a balance of rear foot pressure to work the edge, front foot for course holding.

If all goes according to plan you'll be up on your board and planing, skimming across the surface of the water with the board slightly leaning onto its upwind edge to work against the kite's pull. It may take a few attempts to get right. There are a couple of things to avoid that will make learning the water start easier. Don't try with too big a kite size or too much power on your first few attempts – if you haven't yet got used to big power you'll never get up; don't bring the kite too low or too far into the wind window as it will give too much lateral pull and heave you forwards, straight off your board.

Learning the water start is, for obvious reasons, fundamental to all your future activity. You will need to use this technique whenever you fall in the water, once you've re-launched your kite, if that has ended up in the water too. Practice water

Beach Start

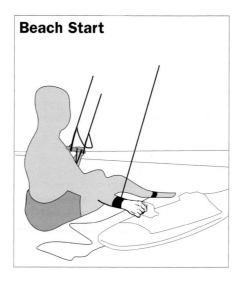

starting to both sides, regular and goofy, so that you're comfortable getting up and planing in either direction.

Beach Start

Once you feel confident about the water start you can think about making your start closer to dry land – what is known as the beach start. If you are fortunate enough to be riding a shallow water lagoon you may not have enough depth for lying down and will need to have this as an alternative. It's much trickier to get right because it all happens quicker but it's a much cooler, cleaner departure. For this one you need knee-depth water at

most and to have your board, as before, in front of you, pointing across and slightly down wind. You should be hooked onto your harness on the small harness loop. Then:

■ Put your kite up at the zenith and put your front foot in its strap.

■ Get some power back into your kite by bringing it slowly down the wind window. You will feel the power come on and yourself being gradually lifted.

■ As the power in the kite lifts you up, swing it over towards the side of the wind window you want to move towards, at the same time stepping up onto the board with your rear foot, placing it as close to the strap as you can get it so you get moving quickly.

■ Keep the kite powered-up and moving towards the edge of the wind window to gain apparent wind and even more power.

■ Once you're moving forward, stable and powered-up, you can get your rear foot properly into its strap, adjust your body position, and dig the back edge in to work the board back upwind slightly.

■ With both feet in their straps you can concentrate on planing with the kite locked in position at the edge of the window. It's all in the feet again.

If the wind is strong enough, with a four line you can virtually lock it in position at 45 degrees to the water and concentrate on steering, holding your line across wind by working the edge, with the board. Apparent wind works again and the more you can steer the board across and slightly upwind, the faster you will be able to go. If you want to try to get further upwind, with the water to lever against, you can bring the kite further down the wind window to power up, at the same time using heel pressure to carve the edge into the water, wedging the board and pointing it more upwind. Once you're pointing the right way take the kite slightly back up the edge of the window and press with the front foot on the board to straighten up again.

If the wind is on the light side for your size of kite, you will need to work it more using the S pattern. The effect of this on the board is that as the kite descends towards the bottom of the S it picks up power, accelerating towards the bottom edge of the window. The rider must work the backside edge and steer upwind to avoid catching up with the kite, causing it to lose power and possibly collapse. The

▶ *Powered up and working the edge to stay upwind*

kite will gradually lose power as it climbs back towards the top of its S, before the cycle begins again. You need to find a good rhythm of powering up, increasing speed, turning upwind and then gradually straightening again as the kite climbs. The weaker the wind, the more exaggerated the S of the kite and weave pattern of the board.

Of course you could use a big floaty board in light wind but riders are generally happier waiting on the beach for the wind to build up so they can get out and go bonkers, massively powered up on their tiny trick boards. Indeed there are even people who have succeeded in stacking two LEI kites together, giving a total sail area of over 25 square meters, and being able to get upwind in as little as 5 knots because of it. Old habits die hard, it seems; I wouldn't mind betting that the person who thought of this started off their power kiting career flying Flexifoil power kites.

Changing Direction Or Turning Around

These are conflicting views of an old conundrum but what we're talking about is that strange nautical concept, jibing or gybing. Thankfully for beginners, it's almost obsolete now, but there was a time when jibing was a fundamental part of the whole package. Nowadays it's possible to learn kiteboarding on a twin

> **The skills you learn will benefit wave and frontside riding later. Even on flat water it's really good fun doing a hard carve jibe on a twin tip or wakeboard and popping the board back round on the exit.**
> CHRIS CALTHROP Flexifoil team kiteboarder

> **Jibing is almost over. Most people today have a twin tip board which makes it really simple and easy to turn round.**
> MARK DOYLE Slingshot International Team pro kiteboarder

tip board, goodbye jibe. But if you're using a directional board for learning (not a bad idea) it's essential. Even for those of you riding twin tips it's still a cool maneuver you can use and that it would be useful to know. Riding a wake board with full-foot or ankle bindings or twin tip means that jibing presents a different set of issues as it will leave you riding backside on the frontside edge, that is to say, leaning forward rather than back and flying the wing over your leading shoulder. What we're interested in is the standard directional jibe and the frontside twin tip alternative, which is in fact an advanced maneuver – don't be disappointed if you don't get it straightaway.

In one sense the directional jibe is similar to the basic windsurfing jibe: you've got to turn the board and get over onto the other edge to go back the way you

came. But there all similarity ends as, with no fixed mast to hold onto, it becomes a question of balance and timing to turn the board, step over into the foot straps on the other side and resume planing, all the while balancing yourself against the pull of the kite. There's a potentially scary moment when you're out of the straps and face on to the kite, and timing is crucial. You are strongly advised to try the foot movements several times on your board on dry land until you're confident of them. No tricky foot movements are needed on your twin tip, which in principle makes it easier. However, it has the added technicality of needing a big shift of body weight and the body must be positioned leaning forwards rather than backwards, which is more natural. These are the instructions if you want to change direction:

135

1 You're planing along with good forward speed. The board is flat rather than riding on the edge. Unhook from your harness, keep your kite high and get ready to move. But there is no need to unhook on your twin tip!

2 Take your rear foot out of its foot strap and put it just in front of the strap. Flex and press with your front foot to tilt the board forwards more, pressing the rail into the water. Bend your rear knee at the same time to make the tilting smooth, firm, and even. Twin tip riders initiate the turn by pressing more with their front foot toes to bring the board flat, body position more upright.

3 Control the tilt of the board with your free (rear) foot. Steer the kite straight up to the zenith where it will stay during the next phase. Hold the control bar or handles at arm's length and start to turn the board physically with your feet. Twin tip riders can shift their weight forwards more and start using toe side pressure to turn the board ready to power up again quickly; directional riders still have one crucial phase to complete as described in the next three steps...

As the board turns you find your body coming round to ride backside, back towards the kite. Keep the kite at the zenith.

4 Now take your front foot out of its strap and bring your rear foot up so that you're

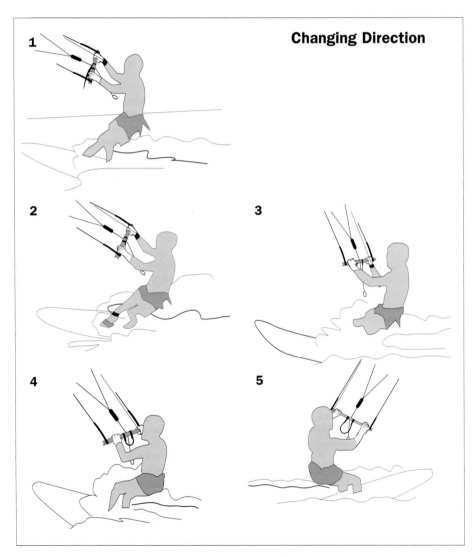

Changing Direction

1

2

3

4

5

standing, feet parallel and pointing forwards along the board, just beside or behind the front foot strap.

Keeping the kite at the zenith still, quickly reverse the positions of your feet, putting what was your rear foot into the front strap and your other foot into the rear strap.

Whichever way you got to this point you will now need to power the kite up again quickly to drive through the final part of the turn and be able to work the edge to hit that return run.

5 Before you've got the board through its turn, start the kite moving again downwards into the power zone and towards the edge of the wind window you want to move towards for your return run. You'll have lost speed through the turn and powering up again quickly will help prevent the board wallowing. Lean back over your heels or forwards over your toes on a twin tip, to counteract the pull, and off you go again in the opposite direction. Twin tip riders can simply pop their board back round to ride normally again at almost any point after the jibe.

▶ *Toe-side jibing on a twin tip board*

If you want to have the best chance of hitting a good jibe, avoid:

■ not having enough forward speed going into the maneuver
■ not tilting the board enough
■ allowing power back into your wing too soon, resulting in wipe-out
■ not getting your wing going soon enough to power up again, resulting in sinking.

It's a lot to think about and may take you many attempts to get right. The idea is to make it one continuous and smooth movement, turning the board quickly and getting it moving again before it has a chance to slow and sink.

The chances are that you'll be learning on a twin tip board, in which case there's no jibe needed. That was very much the reason they were created: first to eliminate the tricky stage of jibing as a hindrance to progress (a lesson learned from windsurfing), second to facilitate an altogether trickier (as in range and variety of tricks) style of riding for people who progressed beyond the basic level. But you still need to know how to turn around. In fact we described almost the identical sequence for kite landboards in Chapter 6, those being twin tips too. It's a logical process of maneuvers with the kite and board, the object being, over time, to learn to change or reverse direction without coming to a complete stop, keeping yourself powered up and moving. One step at a time however... This is what you do if you want to turn around on a twin tip board:

- As you're planing along, steer the kite up the edge to top center window, where it will lose power and you will slow down.
- As you slow down almost to a stop, shift your weight towards the center of the board, in a more upright body position, ready to go back the other way.
- Before you feel the board stop completely, steer the kite towards the edge you want to move towards, diving it down in the window and bracing your body for the power coming back on.
- Lock your kite in position, lean back, find your balance and pressure points, and away you go, leading with your other foot.

If you can start up, plane on the board, work the edges to go upwind a bit more and turn around to get back to your start point, you've got all the basic maneuvers you need to start out in the exciting world of kiteboarding, the most exhilarating new extreme sport around. Now it's practice,

▶ Kite high and stable: Perfect for first jumps
▶ Far right: Advanced trickery: Toe-side grab

practice, practice. It's good to go solo riding but you will learn a lot by riding with other, more experienced riders, watching what they do, asking them how they do it. With your own growing level of skill and experience and the benefit of theirs you will progress quicker and soon be ready for some more radical and dangerous moves.

Stopping

It is to be hoped that you are only going to need to stop for one reason – when you want to get back onto dry land. It may be that other emergencies dictate that you stop out on the water. A dead stop will sink you, for sure. Even on a larger-volume directional board the chances are you will be down in the water, although your kite should be safely positioned and you shouldn't need to water launch it. You should be hooked on to your short harness loop or de-power system. To stop:

- As you are reaching across the wind (and are nearing the beach), start steering the kite up the edge of the wind window to lose power and slow down.
- At the same time start leaning back to work the rear edge and turn your board upwind.
- Steer the kite to the zenith, and when the board is pointing upwind press with your front foot to bring the board and yourself upright.

- Step off the board quickly and, keeping the kite stable at the zenith with one hand, pick up your board with the other and leave the water, detach yourself from the board and follow the normal procedure for an assisted landing.

The idea is to stop close enough to dry land to be in shallow water and step off the board. If you have to execute your stop in deeper water, obviously you won't have that luxury. But your kite should be stable up at the zenith and it will be another chance to practice your water re-start. It's all a question of timing, as usual. With skill and practice you'll be able to stop suddenly, but always be careful as you steer the kite up the window not to get it too far behind you, as it will either pull you over, or power up, in which case you'll be heading for an unexpected jump. Stopping at exactly the right place on the edge of the beach is an acquired skill. Whatever type of board you're on, don't approach your landing spot with too much speed; always err on the side of caution.

Jumping

It's one thing checking out the great photos in kiteboarding magazines and books such as this, checking out what the pros are up to on the latest videos and DVDs, but it's quite another actually

" **You need good wind, a fast efficient kite, a thin board... and nerve. Send it!** "

CHRIS CALTHROP Flexifoil team kiteboarder

witnessing a skillful rider (better still a big competition) hitting some big airs. As soon as you see it, you know you want to give it a go. It's slick, it's cool, it's totally impressive and the hang time seems to go on for ever. With power control a rider can even turn the power level up while in the air to extend a jump and with tricks besides. Watching the likes of Mark Doyle, Will James, Adam Koch, Sky Solbach and co. flying past, 30 feet above the water, upside down, is a huge attention grabber and is one of the main reasons so many people want to learn the sport.

There are three distinct phases to each jump: preparation and getting airborne, being in the air, and landing. It may take longer to learn the final element and you must be prepared once again for a lot of falls and water–drinking – having just learned how to ride well enough not to. No gain without pain. Even when you've learned how to do the whole thing it won't stop there because, once you prove to yourself that you can do it, you'll want to

◀ *Aerial handle-pass, high level skill and danger*

keep going for bigger, better, more complicated jumps. And that generally means big wipe-outs. At least as a kite-boarder you've got the cushioning water to land in rather than a hard surface to slam into. Nevertheless, be careful – that water can still seem hard as concrete and hurt a great deal if you hit it at speed.

For your first attempts it will be better if you're on flat water rather than waves or a swell. Learn how to jump properly first; you can start playing trampolines with the water contours later on. As ever, you'll be wanting a smooth wind, strong enough to get you off the water but not so much that everything happens too fast or too hard. Try with a medium-sized kite while you get used to the mechanics, technique, and sensations. Remember, this is pretty much maximum danger: in the air, over water, powered by a big kite and not 100 per cent in control of what happens next, however good you are. It's better to be hooked onto the short harness loop or de-power system during your first jumps. It allows you to control the power before and during the jump and makes it simple to let go of everything if you get into difficulties in mid

jump. Fixed into the long loop, you can't control it and will therefore have maximum power all through the jump. If you're riding with a two-line kite you should unhook altogether for exactly that same safety reason.

Jumping almost always moves you some distance downwind during the time that you're in the air: the bigger the jump, the greater the downwind travel. Be ready for this – make sure you've got a clear zone at least three kite-line lengths downwind before you start your attempts. You should be clear of other riders or water users but also clear of rocks, moored boats, the beach itself, piers, jetties – anything that can pose a potential risk. For a cool jump you need a combination of board speed and good timing, then:

■ **Steer the kite low down (30 degrees) on the edge of the wind window so that you're as powered-up as possible and sailing slightly upwind, pressing hard with your heels to work the edge in the water. You need a good body position to get ready to go airborne, knees bent, body flexed and braced, ready to spring.**

■ **Keep working the edge so as not to lose any speed. Start steering the kite so that it comes slightly back into the wind window, pulling very slightly with the side**

141

of the bar attached to the top wing tip.
- As you do this try to relax some of the pressure on the board so you are less on the edge and more on the flat of the board. Keep moving the kite towards center top of the wind window, pointing straight up.
- Keep working on the board until the pull of the kite in center window is too much to hold. Now, spring into the air letting the kite pull you off the water as you do so. The kite should still be in center window.
- All being well, you are now airborne and will feel the lift effect of the kite. Enjoy every second but keep a careful eye on your kite and make sure it stays where you put it. Don't get it moving towards the edge again too early or you'll have a very hard fast splashdown; keep it as directly above your head as possible.
- Get back into a good braced, flexed body shape for the landing, which is coming up quickly. The kite may well be a little behind you now and it's time to get it back into meaningful action. Don't let it go too far behind you. Pull slightly on your forward hand to start bringing it forwards in the window and have a look to make sure it has started turning. Getting power back in the kite at the right moment results in a softer landing; too much leads to a hard, fast landing.
- Brace yourself for splashdown. Watch the water as you approach to spot that landing

> " It depends on the kite you have. If it's a medium aspect ratio, with 10 knots of wind at water level it won't take much effort. Even with a modern high-aspect ratio, big hang time should be OK. My opinion? If you're still concerned about water re-launching you probably shouldn't be too worried about your kite's hang time. In other words, don't get ahead of yourself... "
> **ADAM KOCH Naish Kites international team pro kiteboarder**

and if you think you're going too fast, with the kite pulling more than you'd like, try to place the board so that it's pointing slightly downwind to lose a bit of speed. If the opposite happens, and you land heavily with little power, dig your rear edge in, steer the board as upwind as possible to try to power the kite up quickly by bringing it low in the window then powering upwards to lift yourself up and get moving again. Bend your knees on landing to absorb any impact and get yourself planing again quickly.

The trick with learning to jump is having the correct kite size up: too big and you won't be able to maneuver it quickly enough, too small and it will be too fast. When you get it right and you start nailing the whole jump, you really are on the way to maxing your sensations. If it's that good to watch, imagine what it must feel like up there on the board.

But don't stop there. You can learn how

to control the power of your jumps to go higher or lower, keep practicing your wing control to get the best possible landings and go for bigger and better jumps. Then you begin throwing in some tricks, starting with some basic grabs, perhaps, and then see where you go after that. It won't be too long, I'm sure, before you're hitting those big upside-down numbers, some rotations perhaps...

Water Re-start

As if it hasn't been mentioned enough already, don't forget you're going to do a lot of falling off your board while you learn how it's done and indeed afterwards if you start progressing on to big jumps and tricks, with a big likelihood that the kite will come down too at some point. So it's imperative that you know how to re-start in water. In fact kiteboarders rarely go more than a few hundred meters offshore, so swimming back in is no great issue. It is very tiring but, as you'll have to dry out your kite before you start again, you'll have a bit of recovery time once you're back on dry land.

There's a strong argument that using an inflatable kite makes you lazy and doesn't place enough emphasis on learning to keep it in the air even during crashes. Certainly the idea is that once you progress beyond learner status the water re-launch shouldn't be needed anywhere near as often. A lot, clearly, is going to depend on what type of kite and what line set-up you're using. If you're using a ram air kite, already your chances of successfully re-launching are about 70 : 30 at best. And if you're using a two-line set-up to fly your ram air kite you're almost certainly looking at a swim back unless you're very lucky and very quick. The problem is that as soon as water gets inside the wing through the vents, or the cloth is soaked from being down on the water too long, it becomes virtually impossible to re-launch. That goes for four-line riders, too. But at least they have a chance either to reverse launch or launch in the normal way, depending on how the kite has landed.

Whichever type of kite you're flying when

▶ *Kite down and time to practice a water re-start*

you end up in the water, it may be as a result of a wipe-out during which you've let go of your kite and come off your board, so the first stage is to recover your equipment. If it was a big wipe-out you might well be winded and need a few seconds to get your breath and bearings back. It's going to be hard work to re-launch, specially if there are waves and you keep getting a face full of water. The first thing to check once you've got your bearings is how your kite has landed. It could be in any kind of position: leading edge up, leading edge down, on its back, face towards you, face down or away, or in a complete heap because you activated your safety system.

Recover your control bar or handles using the leash if you've let go of them and make sure the lines are not snagged around your legs or anything else that could affect re-launch. Check where your board is – not too far away if you've got your leash properly attached. The kite will normally drift downwind of you on the water. You should still be hooked onto your de-power loop; if you aren't, do so now.

If your ram air four-line kite has landed leading edge up, you should have little problem launching it in the normal way, unless it then falls face down on the water. With the bridles submerged under the kite, you're done for. During a

▲ *Mauricio Abreu shows what's possible*

standard re-launch you may need to swim backwards to help get enough tension on the lines to lift the off but, once launched, it will power up quickly, especially if it has drifted near center window. Quickly steer it to a safe position at the edge or zenith of the wind window so you can get ready for your water start.

It's quite common for the kite to land leading edge down. If you're using a four-line set-up you can try to reverse launch in the normal way. Again, if the kite falls face down at this point, you're in for a swim. If it falls on its back, a quick pull

on the rear lines should get it upright again, on its leading edge. Then:

■ **Pull back on the bottom of the handles to put tension on the rear lines. You may need to try to swim backwards as you do this until there is sufficient tension for the kite to develop enough lift to start reversing. Pull back equally on both sides.**

■ **As the kite lifts off backwards and reaches a height above the water where you are sure you can turn it, pivot one handle so the rear line is pushed forwards and the front line has tension on it.**

■ **The kite should turn around its center point**

until the leading edge is pointing straight up. Pivot the other handle so that both front lines are pulled to move the wing up the window away from danger. Steer it to a safe position at the zenith, where you can get ready for your water start.

In both cases, if the kite is directly down-wind of you it may be a good idea to re-orient it closer to one edge so as to avoid full and unexpected power up at the moment of take off. This can be done by either swimming to one side or by pulling on one handle only to move the wing across before you re-launch.

It's quite different water launching an

inflatable or bubble kite. Even so it's certainly no cakewalk and just because you've bought an inflatable doesn't mean it does it all automatically. There's still lots to learn and you've got to get it right. There's a "dead" position from which there's no recovery, no matter how much you spend on equipment and courses. If the kite is down on its face, leading edge down in the water so you can see the back of the wing, then no amount of water re-launchability is going to help.

From any other position down on the water, you're in with a more than even chance. One factor to consider is the kite's aspect ratio. Some competition-standard, high-performance inflatable kites are enormously elongated (have high aspect ratio) and are generally more difficult to re-launch because of it. A good beginner kite would be more rounded (have low aspect ratio), making it easier to get onto one wing tip, a crucial phase in the re-launch.

Inflatable kites can occasionally re-launch themselves when you're not expecting it, so watch out for that first and foremost. Technically, it's feasible to reverse a four-line kite off the water but in reality this is extremely difficult, almost to the point of impossible.

If the kite has come down on its trailing edge then it's a simple job to re-launch by pulling back on the control bar. Be aware of the kite's position in the wind window, however. Too much power could be a problem so try to get off-wind by swimming to one side or by pulling on one side of the control bar only at first to move it towards the edge before you attempt the re-launch.

Likewise if the kite is down on one side or wing tip. You will need to steer the kite to one edge (the one that the leading edge is facing) first:

- Pull back on the side of the control bar attached to the upper tip and swim in the opposite direction to which you are steering the kite at the same time.
- When the kite nears the edge of the window you can pull on the lines attached to the upper tip to lift it off the water.
- Then steer it carefully up the edge of the wind window to the zenith (remembering to push forward with your control bar to help the kite climb).

The tricky one is if your kite comes down leading edge down, face towards you. At this point you have to try to get the kite to fall over on one tip, but this is easier said than done. If there's a good wind blowing the wing will keep powering up and pulling you downwind. Fortunately, sophisticated kite design means they are built with easy water re-launch in mind, and lots of kites are relatively easy to get onto one tip. Nevertheless you must try to de-power your kite by swimming towards it and taking tension off the flying lines:

- Swim towards the kite until enough tension goes from the flying lines for the kite to fall onto its back. Be aware of where your flying lines are so as not to get them snagged on you or your board.
- Pull on one side of your control bar to bring the kite up onto one tip or side. This may require swimming backwards a little to get tension on that side.
- Once the kite is on one tip, steer it to the side you have chosen and don't change your mind as this will simply prolong the whole process. Pull back on the lines attached to the upper tip. The kite may move slowly so be patient.
- Once it reaches the edge of the wind window, a further pull on the lines attached to the upper tip will lift the kite off the water.
- Steer your kite carefully up the edge of the wind window to the zenith and get ready for your water start.

Whichever type of kite you're using, water re-launch is a relatively advanced technique so you may not manage it right

away. It's a good idea to practice in shallow water near the shore until you're confident you can get a good percentage (50 per cent or more). That way you'll be ready when it does happen half a mile offshore and won't be so daunted by the prospect. Be ready for the kite to behave differently after being down in the water. It'll be heavier and less responsive to begin with, until it dries again, which is best done by keeping it in the air and moving.

With your kite back up at the zenith it's time to get on your board again using your water start. You've already done the hardest part, recovering your kite, and if all goes according to plan you'll quickly be up and planing again. You may not be so fortunate, and so the final part of your basic kiteboard training is what do to do if it all goes horribly wrong.

Getting Back To Shore

It's going to happen sooner rather than later. As usual, there's a simple step-by-step procedure, one that you definitely need to practice several times in shallow water before it happens in choppy sea further out than you care to imagine. In those circumstances, if there's no rescue boat around, it becomes not so much a question of getting started again as saving your life. Your board will be on the end of its leash and will be very useful presently for getting everything back to land. For now you need to concentrate on finding your control bar or handles and making sure the flying lines aren't twisted around your legs or the board under the water. Then:

- **Once you've found the control bar or handles, start winding in the flying lines while swimming slowly towards your kite. Wind as far as just in front of the kite.**
- **Now straighten out the kite. If it's an inflatable the first thing to do is deflate the vertical battens using the valves, starting with the tips and working your way inwards to the center one last. Then deflate the leading edge. Each time you deflate a tube, take care not to allow any water in. Likewise, once they're deflated, close the valves properly.**
- **From this point the procedure is the same for ram air or inflatable. Place the control bar on one tip and roll the kite up around the control bar. If rolling up a ram air try to squeeze the air out through the vents as you roll to make a less bulky package.**
- **With the kite rolled you can put it on your board. Take your harness off so the hook doesn't cause discomfort while lying on the board; attach it to the rear strap, lie on the board and paddle back in.**

Once you're back to dry land it's time to re-inflate those tubes or dry out your ram air and make a quick check that the flying lines are OK before getting yourself re-launched and re-started. It's possible to buy a kiteboarding backpack or waist pouch to wear while you're riding. Either of these would be a useful accessory to have during this exercise because you can put the kite in the pouch or pack, attach the harness to it and it to your rear foot strap and paddle your board in towing the whole lot behind you. You can practice all this on those days when there's enough wind to fly the kite but not to get up on the board. Make sure it's second nature to you before you have to cope with this in less forgiving circumstances.

Basic Rules For Kiteboarding Safety

As mentioned, when you start playing around with the awesome power of traction wings and then add the extra mystery ingredient of water, it's a recipe for extreme fun but also for extreme danger. Safety first, second and third is very much the order of the day because if it ever appears that kiteboarding is unnecessarily risky there will be calls for it to be prohibited.

Many of the international, national, and regional associations quickly took on the role of educating riders and training trainers as soon as the new sport started getting attention and attracting newcomers. They have all been working to a similar set of basic safety guidelines, which apply to riders of all skill levels but specially to beginner riders. The British Kite Surf Association (BKSA) was one of the earliest to be formed. It identified a number of basic skills a rider should have acquired in order to move successfully onto the water. With thanks to the BKSA, those guidelines are reprinted here in full.

The BKSA Safety Guidelines

Kiteboarding is an extreme sport and is therefore potentially dangerous to both the kiteboarder and others. The overriding need is for rider responsibility. It shouldn't put anybody off or sound too officious, but with so many newcomers to kiteboarding it was felt necessary to lay out a complete set of safety guidelines. For everyone's future enjoyment of this fantastic sport, please read, digest and adhere to all relevant safety guidelines, starting here...

Kiteboarding should not be attempted without appropriate instruction.

The minimum competence levels are considered to be:

Level 1: Kite Flying Skills
- Understand all aspects of safe handling of kites on land and water.
- Able to launch and land (unaided) on a specified spot on land.

Level 2: Basic Water Skills
- Body surfing with kite (along and back to shore).
- Water launching onto board.

Level 3: Basic Kiteboarding Skills
- Getting on a board and travelling a distance under kite power.
- Emergency stop on water – getting off the board quickly and stopping with the kite aloft.
- Returning to base on land either by kiteboarding, paddling or body surfing home.

General safety guidelines
- Stay clear of power lines and overhead obstructions.
- Never fly a kite in a thunderstorm.
- Always inform the Beach Warden, Life Guard or Coast Guard of where and when you will be kiteboarding (kites hitting the water can look like planes crashing to the uninitiated). Beaches, airspace and the ocean environment belong to everyone and must be kept safe, clean and free.

Kite contraindications
- If you cannot walk backwards when the kite is flying at minimum power (overhead) the kite is too big or the wind is too strong.
- Never tether yourself to the kite with a closed system. Only use open quick-release harness systems if any.
- Never attempt kiteboarding if you don't have a good level of kite flying experience.

Site etiquette
- Do not lay kite lines across anyone's path.
- Do not launch or land in crowded areas.
- Always announce you are launching a kite.
- Select a safe launching site.
- Prevent kites from re-launching by weighting down with sand or other ballast.
- Disable unattended kites.

Water
- Never kite surf in areas congested with swimmers, boats, other craft and obstacles.
- Never go out on the water without telling another person where you're going.
- Always maintain a downwind safety buffer zone to allow for being pulled downwind.
- A kiteboarder must know the rules of the sea, including navigation laws, and abide by them at all times.
- Instruction must be taken from an experienced kiteboarder before attempting kiteboarding for the first time.

149

- A kiteboarder should be fit and healthy and over 18 years of age (under 18s must provide a written parental permission).
- If going off shore, kiteboard in pairs or with a rescue boat in attendance.
- Never kiteboard in conditions which are too extreme for you or your equipment.

Equipment
- All manufacturers' instructions and safety guidelines must be read and followed with particular regard to the limitations of the product.
- Equipment must be checked regularly for wear and tear and repaired or replaced before going onto the water.
- Always use adequate safety equipment.
- Be safe – wear a helmet.

Essential Equipment

The full list of kiteboarding essentials depends to a large extent on where you're going to do most of your riding. The air and water temperature will make a huge difference, for example, to the thickness of your wetsuit, and indeed whether you wear one at all. But suffice to say there's an armory of other pieces of equipment aside from the board and kite that you'll need to have before you can get out on the water, wherever you're planning to plane:

- Harness – Absolutely essential. Generally available in two styles, the belt harness and the seat harness. The former fits around the waist and the other is a full crotch fit. The seat version helps get the center of pull and balance much lower, making boarding more stable.
- Wetsuit – Absolutely essential. Available in different thicknesses (3–7 millimeters) depending on how cold it's likely to be; 3–5 millimeters is the most common. They come in different leg and arm lengths with a shorty suit in 3 millimeters being the kind of thing for warm-water riding. Even in tropical waters, if you plan to ride all day a shorty suit can protect you from crash landings and hypothermia. There are different fits for men and women. Always try on in the shop before you buy. If they won't let you, go somewhere else.
- Flotation or buoyancy – Absolutely essential. Some belt-style harnesses now incorporate buoyancy.
- Crash helmet – Absolutely essential. There's no excuse for not wearing one.
- Board leash – Attaches the board to your ankle or rear of your harness via a Velcro strap fastening and length (6 feet approx.) of vinyl cord. You can ride without one if you like but you're going to be chasing your board all over the place.
- Safety system – Absolutely essential. Comes as standard with most kites nowadays.

- Wind meter – Expect to pay handsomely for any handheld meter with any accuracy.
- Puncture repair kit – Absolutely essential. Like a bicycle puncture repair kit but for the inflatable tubes (bubbles) that are vital to your kite's functioning.
- Basic human repair kit – Plasters, antiseptic, bandages, sling; this is an extreme sport remember?
- Sun block or ultraviolet protection – For those parts of you not covered by your suit and which will be exposed to the elements all day.
- Sunglasses – As above but for your eyes.

That's what you need to get you going. What about all those things that can happen during the day (other than a tube bursting) that you need to cover yourself for? The more you kiteboard the more gear you're going to accumulate for doing different things and the more potential there is for hardware failure to spoil your day out. Here is a list of other items you should consider taking:

- spare flying line sets in case of a damaged or broken line
- spare control bar
- splicing and sleeving kit for making adjustments or repairs to flying lines
- spare fins for your board
- spare straps or bindings

■ toolkit with spare fittings for fins and bindings

■ spare harness (an old one perhaps)

■ different types of board depending on the conditions – a larger volume directional or twin tip for light winds and a wake or mini board for strong winds and flat water

■ a reserve supply of energy bars or drinks in case, as can easily happen, you stay out riding a long time and need to get emergency energy in your body once you're back on dry land

■ a waterproof watch so you can actually keep track of time instead of losing it.

Having dealt with all the important and essential items, it's worth pointing out that kiteboarding, in common with other board and surf sports, is a very style-conscious affair. Clothing manufacturers sponsor the riders up to the eyeballs, fueling the whole thing even further. Sure, there's looking cool during the apres-surf once the water action's finished, but there's a great deal of sartorial splendour out there on the water, too. Large numbers of riders seem to resent the anonymity of the standard dark neoprene wetsuit and you'll find that there are thousands of garments on the rails and shelves to choose from now that will cover your modesty, if that's what you want.

Body Surfing And Dragging

You're going to end up doing some body drag and surf as part of your kiteboarding beginner course. It's good fun, you don't need a board or buggy but you will need a wet suit because dragging your body along through shallow water is just inviting those rocks, razor shells, and other flotsam and jetsam to enter where they're not at all welcome. Those of you using four-line kites will need your harness; this is a great learning phase for how to let yourself be pulled by the kite, how to power up and de-power and the principle of pushing the bar away from you to help it climb. It's also a good way of getting used to flying and working the kites while in the water.

Any stack of kites or single big kite will do the job, and any line configuration. It's not complicated to drag and surf; in fact it's much like skidding on land. It's not too technical to get yourself going and the main thing to avoid is getting yourself out of your depth of water until you're confident of not dumping the kites in the water while body dragging. You might want some kind of flotation jacket to help make sure your body is well up in the water if the kites de-power for any reason.

If you were paying attention earlier on you'll know all about flying a flat figure-eight pattern with your kite slightly above mid window as a means of generating constant pull on dry land. That's what you do to start skidding on the ground and, whereas you lean backwards for a good skid, you're now going to be lying on your front, letting the kites pull you along and keeping your head out of the water at the same time. Start by standing up and, once the power comes on, you plunge forward onto your front, keeping your arms free for steering the kite or wing. The more consistently you can keep the power on, the less water you're going to drink.

There are two ways of flying your figure eight: going down the middle and up the sides (good practice for kiteboarding), or the old kite flyers' system of up the middle and down the sides. That's if you want to go straight downwind, albeit zigzagging slightly. You can try body dragging across the wind, too; if you try flying the figure S we mentioned near the edge of the wind window, you should go further to that side.

Be especially careful when body dragging in coastal water. The safest conditions are sideshore winds, allowing you to go along the shoreline, never getting too far from land and able to leave the water to get

151

back upwind when you need to. Avoid offshore winds as these could drag you out to the danger of the open sea. Light onshore wind is OK, too, although it will be hard work walking out far enough for a decent drag back in through even shallow water flying a big kite. It's perfectly possible to cross rivers, lakes, and reservoirs depending on their size but you need to be sure you have the skill and strength to get across – and some way of getting back again afterwards with your gear.

▶ Body dragging

Where To Go

There are literally thousands of good power kiting spots to visit on the thousands of miles of American coastline both on and off the beaten track. But America's a vast country with a huge interior and large population with no immediate access to a beach site. For pure recreational flying almost any good open site that conforms to all the safety guidelines explained at the beginning of the book will do. For the more serious stuff obviously other criteria, notably the one of having maximum space, and specifically kiteboarding where there is the pre-requirement for water too, will apply.

Once you start getting into buggying or boarding you would be much better off heading for one of the recognized sites where you might well find other drivers around – after all kiting is a social thing. Not only that, your spot may be covered by insurance and or, in the case of kiteboarding, have support boats. People who've been power kiting for a long time will have a good knowledge regarding the best places to go, as well as plenty of little tips and bits of advice about how to improve your enjoyment of the sport. But you might really want to get out on your own 'on safari'. After all, it's a huge country and there's a huge amount to explore. If you do decide to go off exploring, keep safety in mind. Go with a friend or, if you go out alone, remember to let someone know where you're going and when you expect to be back. Carry a cell phone plus food and water in case anything happens.

For a good list of existing 'approved' or simply good sites to buggy and landboard you could start by checking out the AKA website listed in the 'Clubs and Associations' section following.

If anything there's a bit more freedom with kiteboarding. Buggies really need that hard flat sand to run well. Kiteboarders can launch from almost any type of beach with assistance, then once they're out on the water the only worry is landing again! But when you're learning the sport or just progressing from the beginner stage you'll want to use spots with an easy, safe access and preferably some kind of rescue/support boat. Cohabitation with windsurfers, bathers and other water users is an issue. Always check if local restrictions apply. In some cases you may only need to drive another five minutes to find restriction and hassle free facilities. In many places there are seasonal restrictions linked to holiday periods when the beaches and water are simply too busy to use.

A good source of information for where to find good sites is the PASA or IKO web sites. Contact details for PASA (Professional Air Sports Association) and the IKO (International Kiteboarding Organisation) are in the following section. The IKO is an organisation that instructs and coordinates the instruction of kiteboard instructors for inflatable wings world-wide. As such it is a great resource of information regarding where to find kiteboarding schools around the world. PASA is an American organization dedicated to domestic air sports activities.

Many dealers and retailers offer individual after sales classes or formally structured courses which you're strongly advised to take up. And wherever you find a dealer you'll find their customers somewhere nearby who will already know the best places to go and how to do it. Why not think about a weekend or week long course of lessons if available? An intensive course is the best way to learn and it's great fun to go away for the weekend with a group of like-minded people for some intensive amusement and hands-on extreme sport action.

There are dozens of kiteboarding schools to choose from now, many linked to windsurf and other water and extreme sport centers, equipped with rescue craft etc. You'll now find kites in many surf shops with boards and other kiteboarding equipment in many kite shops, many of which, as mentioned, offer tuition. Big holiday companies and countless smaller ones are offering kiteboarding and snow kiting course holidays in various locations around the world.

If the US mainland is well blessed with power kiting sites, so too are many other places around the world. Anywhere with good, big, empty beaches, shallow 'lagoon' water or big waves and regular good strength winds. Lots of exotic warm water island locations that are big for windsurfing are already well established on the kiteboard circuit so you could do worse than start with a trip to Hawaii / Maui, the very nerve center of all things surf. In Europe, the Canary Islands offer great winter warmth and excellent wind and beaches, and France is the biggest European market for wind and water sports. But if you really want to go exotic then why not try New Caledonia in the south Pacific, the Madeleine Islands in Canada, the Dominican Republic, Martinique or Guadeloupe in the Caribbean, the Greek island of Paros, Tarifa in Spain, Australia, New Zealand, Tahiti, Venezuela, Mauritius, Copacabana Rio de Janeiro, Madagascar, Egypt, South Africa..... Many locations now have fully equipped kiteboard schools and/or a well-established primary location plus good information regarding where other spots you can explore.

Clubs, Societies And Associations

There is difficulty in establishing viable national associations for what are still, all things considered, fringe sports such as power kiting, however popular they may appear to be getting.

However, the one area where it does look like something is happening on a national scale is in kiteboarding (including the snow version) where the PASA (Professional Air Sports Association) has taken kiteboarding under its wing (joining hang gliding, paragliding, parasailing, ultralight flight and other potentially fatal sports). They have embarked on a programme of instructor and student certification and are a good point of contact for traction kite programs. They're the only true national training group in the USA at this time. Contact them at :

PASA, P.O. Box 1839,
Nags Head, NC 27959
Telephone : 252-480-1500
www.professionalairsports.org
Also worth checking is the IKO website at :
www.ikorg.com
Kiteboarding being power kiting's brand leader, there are dozens of local groups dotted around the country, far too many

to list here but you may find a contact for one in your area via PASA or on the excellent www.kiteforum.com web site which has all sorts of useful links plus advice on how to access second party liability insurance. There are also dozens of discussion forums on the site ranging over every imaginable topic concerning power kiting where you'll find or can ask for valuable information. Even for those with association phobia, these groups can be incredibly useful in terms of identifying safe local spots, organizing events and dealing with insurance.

As far as buggying and other power kite activities are concerned, the options are somewhat more limited. The nearest you'll get to a national organization is the AKA (American Kitefliers Association) which has been in existence for many years, serving the needs of kite flying generally, all the way from kids' kites to kiteboarding. It's a cover-all group but one which has a couple of relevant specialist subdivisions, one dealing with general land traction kiting and the other with kiteboarding. Contact the AKA groups at:
General contact : www.aka.kite.org
Traction kiting : traction@aka.kite.org
Kiteboarding : kitesurf@aka.kite.org

The AKA also have links to other regional and local groups and are your best point of contact (other than your local dealer) for finding out about activity in your area.

There's also one (inter)national kite buggy event which goes off in America every year, drawing guests from around the world, including regular annual visits from power kite guru Peter Lynn, as well as bringing some of the sport's pioneers out of hiding. It's called the Spring Break Buggy Blast and is held on the salt flats in Nevada where, for ten days every year, kite buggies rule. If you get into the sport it's a must-do event at least once in your life. A visit to the SBBB web site will give you a flavor of the US desert buggy scene generally and contacts for the annual get-together :

www.sbbb.net

Index